THE LiFE MANUAL

THE LIFE MANUAL

*tips, tricks, and techniques for
a stress-free home and life*

Wendy Hobson

ARCTURUS

With acknowledgements to contributions from Michael Johnstone and Jane Maple.

ARCTURUS

This edition published in 2017 by Arcturus Publishing Limited
26/27 Bickels Yard, 151–153 Bermondsey Street,
London SE1 3HA

ISBN: 978-1-78428-714-6
DA005616UK

Printed in China

CONTENTS

INTRODUCTION

'To change your life, you must first change your habits.'

As the old adage goes, it is harder to break a habit than a principle, and that is certainly true of the way we live. We are always busy but there is always something else that needs to be done. We multitask but don't always finish what we are doing. It becomes a habit to stay late at the office, to say 'yes, of course', when we should sometimes be saying 'no'. But why is it that our lives are so much more hectic when we have so many more benefits than our predecessors? In general, we have more opportunities than our parents, let alone our grandparents, more money, more travel options, more entertainment choices and more technology to help us.

And if that sentence doesn't give you a clue as to what I am getting at, just read it again: more, more, more, more, more, more. Every time a technology becomes available to make things easier, we may grasp the opportunity but then we look to whatever is coming next, filling the time almost before it has opened up. We want the latest, the fastest, the most high-tech. Spurred on by peer pressure and our own enthusiasm, the result for many people seems to be that the proverbial hamster wheel just spins faster and faster.

And sooner or later, we'll flop exhausted at the bottom and everything will grind to a halt.

Well, that's the negative scenario – there are alternatives.

If we continue to spend our lives with our eyes on the horizon, then it's no wonder we trip up. So the purpose of the range of diverse information in this handy little book is to help us to re-focus, to encourage us to enjoy what we do and how we live and to cut out that constant striving for something else. In some ways, we'll look back to less complex times and values that made life simpler. But in other ways, we can embrace the technology at our fingertips. It's not about wanting to go back to the 1950s – there was plenty wrong with life then. It is about making life good in the twenty-first century.

And that means making some changes, which may not be easy at first. Different people will want to be more or less drastic and that's the first lesson: you don't have to do what everyone else is doing – it is up to you to find what suits you best.

However far you want to take it, simply learning to slow down a little and live at a more manageable pace will help you to reduce stress and enjoy your life more fully. First, look at the areas of your life where you feel you need to make changes, start slowly with small adjustments that are easy to implement and just watch the benefits to your well-being.

The straightforward hints and tips in this book apply common sense to find simple solutions to common everyday issues. They are all about removing potential problems before they occur and finding the wisdom to follow a less stressful path. They can help you to:

- cast off the clutter that is holding you back;

- learn to appreciate the present moment;

- have more respect for your environment and be mindful of its precious resources;

- look after yourself and stay healthy;

- re-assess what you eat and drink and understand the fundamentals of a healthy diet;

- make your household chores simpler and more manageable;

- cultivate and enjoy your garden;

- make simple repairs around the house.

That's a lot to get through in a small guide, so we need to apply our common sense and – to borrow a tagline from an expensive and very successful brand – just do it!

Starting with a clean slate

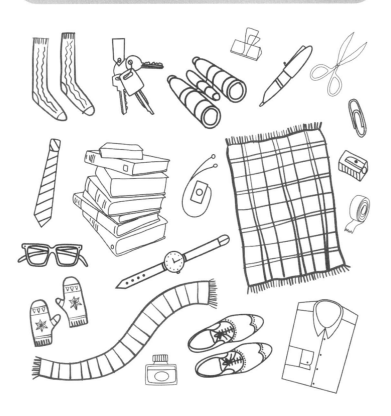

How to rid yourself of the clutter that's holding you back

The idea of decluttering is not new, but its popularity has grown because it makes sense and it is effective. If you are surrounded by mess and muddle, by things you don't really need and that are just getting in the way, it is impossible to get on with life efficiently. Imagine trying to get from one side to the other of a crowded storeroom, filled with old furniture, boxes, piles of magazines and odd-shaped items you don't even recognize. It would not only be hard work physically – clambering over, under and around things – but tiring mentally, too – making sure you don't trip up or break something along the way.

That's what your clutter could be doing in your life – blocking the way to where you should be going.

One person's treasure might be another person's clutter. Only you can decide how drastic you want to be once you decide to declutter. If you find this whole process somewhat daunting, then start small and work gradually. If you are really up for it, hire a skip! Either way, your objective is simple: to get rid of anything that is surplus to current requirements and that doesn't make any contribution to your life, then to make sure everything you do have is in its rightful place.

HOW IT'S DONE

It's a good idea to give some thought to your procedure before you actually start the process of decluttering.

Have a plan
Firstly, establish a plan. Are you going to set aside a weekend or longer? Are you going to work room by room through the house? Both are sensible options. Don't take on too much at once and end up with the entire house taken apart – that way will just increase your stress. Starting in one room and finishing that room before you go on to another is usually the best way.

Now look at each room in turn and think about the space available and how it can best be organized. What do you want to keep in each room?

You might decide to swap things round so your bedroom becomes a spare room or vice versa. Are the cupboards in the most convenient places? Are you using the cupboards and drawers sensibly? Perhaps a cupboard where you have been keeping towels is more suited to something else. Your plan is bound to change as you work through the clearing-out process but let it evolve as you go along. Before you start the next phase, you might want to look at the section on reorganizing your space (see page 12).

What stays and what goes?

Now establish a rule of thumb to help you decide what to get rid of. It might be things you haven't looked at for 12 months or five years. You might just decide to go on your gut instinct. But only keep things that make a positive contribution to your life.

- They might be useful: cutlery, bedding, cans of beans.
- They might be beautiful: pictures, ornaments, jewellery.
- They might make you look good: clothes, make-up.
- They might bring you happy memories: photographs, gifts.

But they will all make you feel good in some way.

Be conscious of the thought that will inevitably creep into your mind that the thing you are about to discard might come in handy sometime. That 'sometime' is most unlikely to materialize. Do you really want it hanging around until then?

When you get to the kitchen, pay particular attention to the dates on cans and herbs and spices. You may love sage but that jar from 2012 is likely to have all the flavour of cardboard – chuck it (see also pages 89–90). If you are a kitchen-gadget fan, think about how often you use a particular gadget before you return it to the clean cupboard, never to emerge again. If it's clutter – it's not a keeper.

On the other hand, keep any instructions or guarantees you find and put them all together in a folder or box. Once you've finished, go through and chuck out the ones for the digital alarm clock you threw away five years ago and just keep those you might need.

Memories are made of this

Even if you are being drastic, be wary of completely discarding things that might be of value to someone else or provide a record of your past. Your children's old report cards, school photos and the like can be put to one side and perhaps thinned out and sorted to give to them at a later stage as mementoes of their growing up. If you like, you could put significant photos, drawings or certificates in a scrapbook – it is much better than just chucking everything in a drawer, and it makes a great keepsake.

What to do with the clutter

Now decide what you are going to do with your clutter. It may be best to get some strong black plastic sacks for rubbish, bags of a different colour for things to go to the charity shop, and a third type of bag for things you might want to sell on Gumtree, or take to a car-boot (yard) sale. Let's say our solutions are: keep, chuck, sell and charity. If you are going to try to sell some items, allocate a space – well out of the way, perhaps in the garage, if you have one – so you can deal with them later.

Avoid giving your clutter to someone else – unless they are absolutely sure they want it, it is likely to end up as their clutter before too long.

Get to it

Now you can get started – a room at a time. Empty the cupboards one at a time, sort through what's in there and decide whether to keep, chuck, sell or give to charity, item by item. Once you have done that (and it will take some time), take the chuck and charity bags out of the room – better still, take them straight to the recycling facility or charity shop. Take the sell bags to your allocated space and make a date in your diary so you don't leave them lurking there for too long.

Clean the cupboards and put everything you plan to keep back in its new place. Then move on to the next room until you have gone through the whole house.

After all that hard work, you will find you feel a great sense of relief, a clearing of the energies in your living space that will help you feel energized and positive.

DEALING WITH THE 'SELL-IT' BAGS

I hope you haven't forgotten that we left some bags of clutter in the garage, which need to be dealt with swiftly. Ask yourself whether you are really going to sell this stuff. If the answer is 'possibly', 'well, I should do', 'I might make a bit of money', 'when I get time' or 'it's a good idea', load them in the car right now and get them to the charity shop. They are all versions of 'no'.

If the answer is a positive 'yes', then you'll want to decide whether a car-boot (yard) sale or a 'mail-order' option is most suitable for you. Have a look online to see if similar items are available before you make your decision. If so, ask yourself the following questions:

- Are they new or second hand?
- How much are they?
- What is the postage cost?
- Are they fragile, demanding careful packaging?
- Are they heavy?
- Is it better if they are collected?

With a bit more research, you can narrow down your options once more. Anything that is not worth the effort of trying to sell, take straight to the charity shop. With anything that is worth posting on a national or local website, take a few photos and list your items straight away. Any items that will be taken to a local car-boot sale should be priced and put in a box while you book your table at the next available event. But do it now.

REORGANIZE YOUR SPACE

Your organizational plan will hopefully have been evolving while you cleared out, with the objective of creating a flow of energy through the house, and you will probably find that there are certain areas that naturally feel more relaxing, invigorating or creative. Pay attention to this in order to make the best use of the space available.

Which room?

Some people will have the option of changing the use of their rooms –
swapping the lounge for the dining room, for example. Others won't be so
lucky. But don't miss this opportunity. You are looking for a logical activity
flow between the rooms that takes advantage of the best natural light at
appropriate times of day, and takes into account the way you feel in each room.

You may be able to do a bit of decorating to help things along. It needn't
be drastic – a coat of emulsion on the walls can completely change the feel of
a room, a few scatter cushions can brighten an area, or some extra lighting
or more subdued lighting can change the atmosphere. A lounge should be
a place where you relax, while a kitchen is more likely to be a creative and
energetic place and needs good lighting. The bedrooms should be cosy and
quiet for sleeping, but also you'll want to inject a personal touch.

The best furniture for the job

Most of us will be making the best of what we have, but sometimes we
carry on using a chest of drawers for bedding, for example, just because we
always have done, when it would be far better holding clothes. Consider
whether the furniture you have is fit for purpose. It may be that a bookcase
in one room could be swapped for a chest of drawers in another. You
may want to buy some boxes or baskets to hold items, or purchase some
hanging storage, for example. Make use of any ways you can to simplify
your storage and access to it, which ultimately makes your life easier.

Look up the storage pages on suitable websites for ideas for storage
options. New products are being invented all the time that might be
just what you need: narrow, roll-out storage units for tall, thin spaces;
hanging storage racks; shelves that fit to doors and wheel out from corner
cupboards, or boxes that fit under the bed. Avoid things that are just
gimmicks and look at the customer reviews, but be prepared to spend a
small amount on such things if they can make life easier.

Use of colour

Colour is vitally important. Think about warm colours – primarily the yellows
and reds – to inject energy and the cool colours – primarily blues and softer
shades – to slow things down. Most people choose a fairly neutral shade for
the main walls and pick out an accent colour in smaller areas.

If you are making changes, think very carefully about the colour and pattern of long-lasting items such as carpet, chairs or curtains. Choose them first, then work from there. That gives you more scope to change other items before the carpet, for example, wears out.

Plants and flowers

Apart from looking attractive, a few pot plants around the place bring refreshing oxygen into the house. Think about the level of light and direct sunlight in the spot you have chosen and find a plant that will like those conditions. If you try to grow a pot plant in an inappropriate spot, you'll fail.

If you treat cut flowers well, they will also bring their beauty and calming influence into your home.

Carnations and pinks: These will last longer if you put them in lemonade instead of water, changing it every few days.

Chrysanthemums: Plunge the cut ends of the flowers into very hot water for a few seconds and then into cold; they will last much longer.

Cut flowers (mixed): An aspirin or two and a change of water every four days or so will keep most cut flowers blooming in the vase for at least a week (as long as the flowers are freshly cut). All cut flowers will last longer if there are foxgloves in the arrangement.

Daffodils (narcissi): Resist the temptation to include other blooms in a vase of daffodils. They will all die sooner rather than later. But if you feel that you have to, soak them for an hour in separate water, then re-rinse them. And if you add charcoal to the water, your daffs will keep their spring-like bloom longer.

Roses: To make roses open out and last for days on end, clip the stalk, make four tiny upward incisions from the bottom of the stalk towards the bloom, and curl the outer layer upwards, taking care to keep it attached to the stalk. Put the roses in warm water and they will open beautifully.

Tulips: To keep tulips fresh and upright for longer, wrap them in newspaper

up to their necks and stand them in water for several
hours before putting them in a vase.

A PLACE FOR EVERYTHING

Now all your worldly goods need a place to go. Think
logically so items are in the most useful place for you. Group things
together: books in one place, shirts in another. That makes them much
easier to find than if they are scattered in four or five different locations.

The things you use frequently need to be at an accessible level. The best
place for the things you use most often is on shelves that are between knee
level and head height so they are easy to see and use. Save those awkward
cupboards for things you rarely need. Having said that, don't put heavy
things too high for lifting, or so low you find them impossible to move.

Storage tips

Bedding: When you've washed your bedding, fold up the complete set
together and wrap in the duvet cover so they are ready to hand when you
change the bedding.

CD shelf: An average shelf is deep enough to store two rows of CDs. Build a
raised insert half the width of the shelf so that the ones at the back can be
reached easily, or use a ready-made shelf designed for cans.

Hanger bar: If you have a tall wardrobe, you may have room to put a
spring-loaded curtain rail across the wardrobe either above your normal
hanging bar or below your clothes and use it to hang spare hangers that
are not in use.

Hanger hunt: Avoid the annoyance of losing the empty hangers among the
full ones by putting empty hangers back at the end of the row. Make it easier
by always putting them back with the open hook facing away from you.

Keep them together: Some people like to hang clothes in 'outfits', others group colours, many hang trousers, then skirts, then tops together. Find the way that makes it easiest for you to see the clothes you want.

Shorts together: If you hang all your short garments at one end of the wardrobe, the chances are that there will be enough space under them for you to fit a shoe rack or even a small set of drawers.

Slippery shoulders: If you find clothes slip off their hangers, wind thick elastic bands round both ends. That will keep the clothes on the hanger, not crumpled on the floor of the wardrobe. Alternatively, you could bind a piece of velvet ribbon around the hanger so the shoulders don't slip off.

Safety and security
If you have young children – either living with you or visiting – make sure you keep your detergents and washing powders out of the way or in a locked cupboard. Nearly all laundry products are at least mildly toxic – at worst seriously poisonous. So keep them where little hands can't get at them. Similarly, knives and any other sharp objects should be kept safely out of reach, as well as kitchen gadgets such as processors or blenders. There are some more safety tips on pages 47–8.

KEEPING IT TIDY

Having established this feeling of clearing the energies in your home, hang onto it! It's worth trying to keep the place tidy, and you will find it so much easier when everything has its proper place and the space is not enmeshed in unnecessary extras. Make a point of putting things away when you have finished with them, rather than just putting them down anywhere. Clear up regularly. The routine may seem dull but you'll be finished so much more quickly and you'll be so much less stressed.

Every six months or so, go through the process again – although when carried out on a regular basis it doesn't have to be so drastic. Continue the good work of clearing out things you don't need to allow space for the things you do.

DECLUTTER YOUR DIARY

So that's the physical element taken care of. Keep up the good work. What about those wretched 'to do' lists of things you ought to do but just can't quite get round to: sorting out your photo files, writing letters, phoning people you haven't seen in ages.

There are two approaches to this. The first is to decide that you are not going to wait for the 'right moment'; when it pops into your head that you should talk to your mum, auntie, friend, colleague – whoever it is – do a quick time-check (midnight is probably not the best time to call your granny), then just get on and ring them. Do things spontaneously and you should find it very refreshing. Plus, you won't be spending your time writing lists – you'll actually be getting things done.

For some, however, that may be a step too far, in which case a list is still the way to go, just don't make it open-ended. Get yourself a small spiral notebook and use a page for only one or two things so that you can tear them out when you are done. When you write something in the book, put that day's date on the corner of the page and also write down the latest time/date you will complete the task. It may be 'today', 'this week', 'end of March', but don't include anything that you don't intend to do for three months.

If you use an online diary, you can use the 'to do' function, or you could create a calendar just for your 'to do' items and include it in your diary.

DECLUTTER YOUR FINANCES

Finance is a complex area and this book makes no attempt to advise you how to get your finances into shape – that is a specialist task. In the next chapter, however, you'll find some common-sense advice to encourage you to think about whether your finances need the kind of overhaul you have just undertaken on the house.

If so, look at the notes, take the best advice and think about making the best use of your available resources. If you are confident that your income and outgoings are positively balanced – or at least balanced – it takes away yet another potential stress factor.

Living in the moment

HELLO

ADVENTURE

LAUGH

BE WHO YOU ARE

Once UPON A Time

ENJOY

Hope

LOVE

BE BRAVE, BE HAPPY

SMILE

BE JOYFUL NOW

Happy

TODAY IS YOUR DAY

BRAVERY IS BELIEVING IN yourself

DREAM

YOU ARE MY SUNSHINE

JOYFUL

How to cultivate mindfulness to bring you contentment

Mindfulness is a very twenty-first century word, but the concept has been around for millennia. It could be called living in the moment, contentment, hygge, or any number of other things. In essence, it is an acknowledgement that the only thing we can be sure of is the present, so we should live in a way that makes every second count. Make a conscious effort to be aware of – and appreciate – where you are and what you're doing right now.

The past is crucial to who we are now and therefore part of our present and our future. But those things that have happened in the past cannot be changed. Interestingly, though, our memories of those events can, making memory both immutable and unreliable at the same time. Try discussing an event that happened some years ago with your children or with friends and see if you all remember the same things. Consider whether an amusing event you have retold many times at parties hasn't become somewhat exaggerated (I know of a penknife that turned into a machete in only a couple of years).

The future, of course, is totally unknown.

So if we spend too much time looking in either direction instead of focusing on where we are now, and fully enjoying the present without being distracted by the future or the past, we are not going to have all our mental energies available to make the best of our lives.

DEALING WITH THE PAST

While we cannot alter the past, we have already seen that we can be selective in our view of it. That happens naturally. We tend to remember the bigger events rather than the general day-to-day. We are inclined to forget the minutiae – except when they are part of a really important event.

The best possible scenario

All the events that have led to this particular point in time are relevant to how we act now. If a happy home life and good education have instilled confidence and knowledge, it may be that you can look back without regrets and view your past dispassionately. That's brilliant. If so, you might agree with the following:

- You can acknowledge the good and bad things that have happened and see which have strengthened you and the lessons you learnt from them.

- You can recognize the influential people in your life and what they represent to you.

- You can be proud of your achievements.

- You can forgive yourself for things that didn't turn out so well.

How to get there

For those of us with issues in our past of one kind or another, the description above is what we should be aiming for. So it may be that a bit of sifting through the most prominent events in our backstory will be necessary to bring us a bit closer to that enviable position. Remember always that it is not what actually happened but how we view what happened that matters now.

An example: you are not happy in your job – perhaps someone has been promoted above you and you feel that you and the boss just don't get on. You've tried to remedy the situation but nothing seems to work. You decide to leave, but the next job doesn't seem much better. Fortune is just not running your way. You move on again, and this time find a job you like and things improve.

Looking back on that period of your life after a few years, you could conclude that you were hard done-by by two employers and you shouldn't have had to move; it was sheer luck that the final company turned out okay – it could have been the same all over again. That's absolutely true.

However, you could look at it another way. Leaving the first job took courage that you didn't think you had, and made you more realistic when assessing whether to make a go of the second job or to cut your losses and move on sooner than you wanted. In the end, you found a job that fitted your skills and personality because the other two jobs had helped you to define the work that suits you and gave you the confidence to find it.

Get the idea? I don't say it will be easy but if you really look, you can find positives in most events.

Some things are just plain awful

There are, of course, times when truly awful things happen to people. These situations are way beyond the scope of this book. If you are on the road to coping with a major tragedy, then I wish you all the strength you need in your journey, and the support of those around you. Do not hesitate to ask for comfort from the people closest to you and to seek professional help and guidance.

LOOKING TO THE FUTURE

Having looked back, we need to look forward. And because we can alter the future, it is up to us to make the decisions now that will result in the best outcome. And if our attitude to the past is healthy and we are making the most of the present, then we will be in the best position to positively influence our future.

Decisions we make need to acknowledge our strengths because that allows us to take risks from time to time. We should also try to assess our weaknesses dispassionately. Not being particularly adventurous is not a bad thing, it just means you would be better being something other than a polar explorer!

When you look to the future, try to be open to all possibilities. Explore avenues even if you think they may lead to a dead end. If you have come this far, you will be able to learn something positive from your experience whatever happens.

It is important to have dreams of where we might be in the future, goals to strive for and things to look forward to. But an occasional reality check is no bad thing either. If you find the determination to overcome the obstacles and reach an 'unreachable' goal, that's admirable – and extraordinary.

LIVING IN THE PRESENT

So how do we make sure we are living in the present?

Firstly, by knowing that we have come to terms with the past. It is not helpful to blame others or ourselves for mistakes or misdirections, and we cannot change the past. We are here now and the only thing is to move forward. Equally, it is not helpful to keep 'what iffing' – what if I had done this or that? You didn't – you are wasting energy on angst that can't take you anywhere so leave it alone.

Equally, always looking forward to the next thing will take your eye off the good things that you already have. Don't think like an excited and spoilt child at Christmas, who just wants to rip into parcel after parcel without paying any attention to the thoughtful and generous gifts. Everyone needs to 'what if?' about the future to a certain extent. Taking job A will have these pros and cons, while taking job B will have different advantages. But try to make sure – whether you are thinking about real situations or simply daydreams – that you are doing so in a positive way that leads you forward, rather than a negative way that holds you back.

Knowing yourself

If you are not happy in your own skin, you will not find contentment, so be kind to yourself. Run through an assessment of your main personality traits, your talents and limitations. Perhaps there are things you can do to improve on what you don't like, but focus on being content with yourself and making the most of your talents. Just as we did when looking at the job scenario and how we could view it from different perspectives (see How to get there, page 20), look for all the positives, turn your weaknesses on their heads and see the value of those characteristics. Most of all, don't beat yourself up.

Remember that you are just as important as everyone else – no more, no less. So your feelings and opinions are of value. On the other hand, you can go too far the other way. Those who assume that they are the only one who matters or that they don't need to listen to anyone else and always put themselves first are selfish in a negative way. The ideal is to recognize our own worth but also that of everyone else and to be self-aware rather than selfish – this is positive for everyone. And it follows that if you respect yourself and others, you will already have moral principles that mean your actions will be considered and honest.

Many of us define ourselves by our achievements. We have been trained to feel guilty if we aren't doing something useful; we always do the chores before we read a book or watch a film. If you recognize this as you, don't even think about trying to change yourself overnight – it won't happen. But do keep reminding yourself that you don't have to be 'doing' all the time – you can just 'be'. It's allowed!

Appreciating those around you

Even if you are happy in your own company, everyone likes to be with other people. They make the moment special. And if you are mindful of that, you can contribute to making more of every day special for yourself and for those around you.

It starts with old-fashioned courtesy. Some people are dismissive of its importance but it seems to me to be a demonstration of thoughtfulness, and if it is a habit to be courteous to other people, it can make a positive difference to the energies surrounding you. Basically, treat others as you would want them to treat you:

- Say 'please', 'thank you' and 'you're welcome'.
- Don't interrupt when others are speaking.
- Hold the door open for someone else to go through.
- Don't talk with your mouth full.

Please don't think I am talking about the Victorian 'a child should be seen and not heard' type of nonsense. It's just about being aware that being nice to other people usually means they will be nice back to you – that's got to be a win-win.

Organizing your life

A chaotic life with a punishing schedule that allows no time to relax is – surprise, surprise – not conducive to mindfulness. At the other extreme, you don't have to wander around in a daze with no thought for where your next meal is coming from! We all have busy lives, jobs to do, chores to fit in, places to go and friends and family to spend time with.

The important thing is to find the balance so that the elements of your daily life are in proportion. If you work from 8am to 8pm six days a week, for example, then your work is taking up an aggressive part of your life. Think about how that is affecting any time you have left. Are you allowing yourself enough time to relax? Is this a short-term situation and a means to an end? Does this life pattern bring positive benefits? What are your energy levels like at the end of the day? Is this sustainable – for how long?

Ask yourself these kinds of question. It may be that you are happy with how your work-life balance is going and feel you have the time to enjoy the present, even at that pace. Great.

If not, look at the changes you could make to slow things down a bit. Try to create some wind-down time when you don't have anything in particular to do, and enjoy it. You might like to keep a journal of how you feel at various times to help you be objective about your work-life balance and what you most enjoy.

BE MINDFUL OF YOUR FINANCIAL CIRCUMSTANCES

You might think this is a digression but if you are not in control of your financial circumstances, then that could become a constant backdrop and prevent you from valuing each moment – or, indeed, any moment. Charles Dickens expressed the issue perfectly in the person of Mr Micawber, who demonstrated that if your spending was sixpence over your income, the result was misery, while if it was sixpence under, the result was happiness.

If you are having to live on a very tight budget, you will have hard choices to make. You probably won't need reminding that you start with the absolute essentials – rent, utilities, food – and move on from there. Keep a notebook (or a spreadsheet) of all your spending so that you will get a sense of reality about exactly what your expenses are. Perhaps use different colours for essentials, other ordinary items and 'luxuries'. Then you will know where to start cutting. You may prefer to use cash; take out just what is available for the week and when it's gone, it's gone.

The saving habit

If you do find you have something left over at the end of the week, it would be prudent to put it away for when the washing machine breaks down or, on a more positive note, when you can get away for a weekend or treat yourself to something you need. If you really are living up to your income, just put £1 away each week; that should hopefully be affordable. Even that will give you £52 at the end of the year that would otherwise have disappeared into the general pot.

If you have children, encourage them to manage their money. Give them a set amount of pocket money each week and if they want to buy something specific, then they will have to save up for it. Hopefully they will already be helping out around the house, but you might like to designate specific jobs that are worth a bonus: cleaning the car, mowing the lawn, cleaning the windows, and so on.

Wise shopping

There are quite a few ways of making savings when you are shopping (there are more on page 35).

- Look out for special offers and reductions but don't be tempted by things you don't actually need.

- Shop late in the day for food that has reached its sell-by date but is still perfectly fine.

- Use coupons from the newspaper or magazines.

- Use loyalty cards for bonus points.

- Try own-brand products.

Online shopping is convenient and can be economical so do use the options of searching out some bargains on the internet. You also have the second-hand option on sites like eBay, and there are many items to be had at knock-down prices that are just as good as new.

A word of warning, though, because it is easy to get carried away. Each item may be 'only' a small amount of money but if you buy several, they can soon add up.

Credit cards and reasons to be cautious

It is very easy to get a credit card that will enable you to spend not only more than you have now but more than you could ever afford. If you use one to even out your spending, and pay off the whole amount every month, you can smooth out your cash flow, which works to your advantage. However, the credit-card companies make their money on the interest they charge. They only insist on a minimum repayment each month, until you have spent up to your credit limit. But that minimum repayment is an arbitrary percentage – nothing to do with your debt or what you can afford. If you only pay off that amount, or anything less than the whole bill, you will be charged interest on everything left owing, for that month. Any money you do pay, goes to pay off the interest before it starts to pay off the capital, so you can see how easy it is to fall into debt.

If your budget is very tight, it may be better not to have a credit card at all so that you are not tempted to overspend. If you do, set a low credit limit and make sure you are able to pay off the whole amount each month.

Take advice

An independent financial advisor is able to give you impartial advice about your finances and how best to deal with them, especially on major issues, such as pensions. Larger companies may offer their own financial advice service. Charges should be clear upfront, and you should always check an advisor's credentials and perhaps get a personal recommendation.

A financial advisor should be able to advise you about pensions, savings schemes, bank accounts, and generally managing your finances.

For your initial meeting you are likely to need details about the following:

- your income and employment;

- pension, if any;

- your current account, savings accounts, etc.;

- any loans or mortgages;

- regular expenditure;

- children, whether living with you or not;

- any other dependants;

- any State benefits or allowances;

- other financial commitments or income.

Make a will

Talking – or even thinking – about death is the last taboo. But we are all going to die – hopefully later, but we just don't know. However young we are, it will make it quicker and easier to sort out our affairs if we have a will. It's that simple.

A will does not have to be drawn up by a solicitor as long as your intentions are quite specific and the document is signed, dated and witnessed by two disinterested parties. However, many solicitors offer a fixed-price service to draw up and store your will and it is worth considering this option. It is highly advisable if you have children or your affairs are more complicated.

You can choose to make specific bequests, decide who will execute your will, who will inherit, who will be your children's guardian, if you have a family, and so on.

You might also like to take the opportunity to put down your wishes with regard to your funeral: burial or cremation, any religious rites, plus descriptions of any particular readings or songs you would like. It might sound a little morbid but it can actually reduce the impact on your family and make it much easier to talk about. It can also take some of the strain off the shoulders of whoever is left to arrange your funeral if they know what your wishes are. There can be no in-fighting, either, if your wishes are written down for all to see.

It is possible to buy a funeral plan in advance, and this can be a good idea because funerals are expensive and paying upfront can reduce the costs. However, you should look at any plans with very great care as some involve an ongoing regular payment, which may not be cost-effective. If you are over 50, it is possible to make a single, one-off payment that covers the major expenses at today's prices; that may be worth thinking about.

RELAXATION IS WHATEVER YOU WANT IT TO BE

Relaxation means something different to everyone. In the same way that some people enjoy a holiday chilling by the pool for a fortnight, while others prefer to climb a mountain, how you relax and enjoy the moment will be just as different. But what is important is that we all make time to relax in our own way.

You might like to keep a journal of how you feel at various times to help you be objective about your life balance and what you most enjoy. It also helps you focus on the present moment.

Meditation

At one end of the scale, the obvious way to relax completely is through meditation. As a starting point from which you can move on to more practice and study, try finding a quiet and comfortable place, sit down, close your eyes and just breathe. You don't have to sit on the floor in the lotus position – you can sit on a cushion or in a comfortable chair, or you can lie down if sitting up straight is uncomfortable for you. Be conscious only of your breath. Take a deep breath in through your nose, hold for a count of ten, then breathe out through your mouth. Do this ten times and you should feel much more relaxed and in control of the situation.

If you find your muscles are very tense, consciously work through each part of the body, from the feet upwards, deliberately tightening those muscles for an in-breath, then releasing them for an out-breath: feet, calves, thighs, bottom, tummy, shoulders, arms, hands, neck, face. Finally, just relax and breathe for five or so more breaths.

Your concentration should wipe everything else from your mind. It may not do so completely the first time but, with practice, you will improve.

Another way of finding this relaxed state is to concentrate utterly on one small thing, perhaps a flower or even a blade of grass. Focus your attention solely on that until everything else disappears from your conscious thoughts.

Quiet activity

Most people can meditate in the simple way just described for maybe ten minutes a day, but if you simply can't sit still and are itching to do something, then any kind of quiet hobby could become your form of meditation instead. Repetitive activities such as knitting, crochet, wood carving or even polishing the car can help quiet the mind, as can mowing the lawn or taking a long walk or swim. If none of these things appeal, then maybe you like to paint, sew, read a book or do a crossword. If your hobby enables you to blot out everything else, then that's the option for you.

Going for broke

Hopefully even those who enjoy fast-and-furious activities like bike racing or skiing will find the time to meditate for a short while each day to give both body and mind a time to switch off. However, if your favourite activities involve total immersion in what you are doing, then that may be your kind of mindfulness – switching off from everything but what is happening in the moment. Whatever you are doing, the aim is to focus on it totally and value each second.

Having fun

While most of us know what we enjoy, it's worth taking a risk now and again and trying something new that we are not sure about. This stimulates the mind and could lead to the discovery of a hobby that you absolutely love. It can also open up your social life. A friend of mine recently started ballroom dancing and her husband only went along with the greatest reluctance, promising to do one or two lessons as it was so far from the rugby, gardening and travel that he loved. Within a fortnight he was a complete convert.

The other side of the coin, of course, is carrying on with something that you are really not enjoying – perhaps because you went along with someone and don't want to let them down, perhaps for another reason. You need to find a way to extricate yourself without offending or inconveniencing them if you possibly can. Talk to them and explain the situation. They may not be enjoying it as much as you think, they may be happy to go alone, or someone else may have suggested teaming up. Try to banish 'I should' from your thought processes. If you are not enjoying yourself, or at least helping someone else or fulfilling a promise, you are better off somewhere else.

Caring for your environment

How to reduce, re-use and recycle for everyone's benefit

We have looked at how to clear the energies around your home and hopefully you have felt some benefit from that, and also from freeing up your mental energies. Those same energies that run through your life also run through everything around you. You are a part of something bigger and you have your part to play in caring for and maintaining the energies of the planet.

It often seems to us as individuals that we can't do much to change the big things that are going on. Global warming, depletion of natural resources, pollution – these are huge issues. How can small things like taking my bottles to the recycling bank make the slightest difference? The answer is that we all have an impact on our environment and every step we take in the right direction helps. It takes each one of us individually to make a decision to do what we can. The more of us who do that, the bigger the impact. You can't make anyone else change their mind or their behaviour but you can change yours, and that will impact on others as a positive example. If everyone individually maked small changes, then the sum total will be huge. Don't think it's not worth recycling because your neighbour doesn't do it, or it's not worth trying to reduce pollutants from a local factory because so many Chinese factories are belching out smoke. We must all do what we can and travel in hope.

Reduce: Cut down the energy and products we waste, especially items that go into landfill.

Re-use: Look after things so they last longer and find new ways to utilize goods to give them a second life.

Recycle: Collect items for recycling so their raw materials can be extracted and used to make new products.

All three reduce the amount of natural resources we use, reduce the energy consumed in manufacturing and generally increase our respect for the wonderful resources we have access to. If we work together and target these three objectives, then we can make an impact on the environment.

REDUCE

Start by deciding that you are going to think harder about what you waste and what you throw away, and to reduce that amount. While recycling is great, stopping waste by not buying what you don't need is even better because it reduces the energy, manufacturing and transport costs of whatever you bought. You can also look at sensible measures to reduce the amount of energy you consume.

Saving energy

Look at the advice on your energy supplier's website on ways to use your energy more efficiently.

- Put on an extra jumper and slippers if you are cold.

- Close the curtains when it starts to get dark.

- Turn your heating down by a few degrees.

- Turn down the thermostat on your water heater, too.

- Set your heating and hot water on timed programmes. Reduce the time they are on for in short increments and see if it makes any difference.

- Adjust radiator thermostats in individual rooms; you may prefer cooler temperatures in the bedrooms, for example.

- Turn off lights when you are not in the room.

- Make sure you turn off all electrical devices that are not in use. Even leaving devices on stand-by can use a considerable amount of electricity.

- If you need to replace any electrical appliances, make sure you choose one of the most energy-efficient models.

- Replace all your old light bulbs with energy-efficient ones. Although they will cost you more initially, you will save money in the long run.

- Don't have your refrigerator on maximum and make sure that its energy-saver switch is on.

- Wash your clothes on a warm- or cold-water setting.

- When possible, dry your clothes outdoors rather than using a tumble dryer. When you are drying them inside, hang them on a rack rather than a radiator.

- If you can turn off the drying cycle on your dishwasher, do so. Just leave the dishes to dry naturally in the air. The heat from the wash cycle will be enough for them to dry quickly.

- If you have air-conditioning in your home, make sure you replace or clean the air filters regularly.

- Don't fill the kettle – just boil the quantity of water you need.

- Walk short journeys or take the bus or train rather than the car.

- Don't leave the car idling in stationary traffic.

- Car share on regular journeys.

Insulation

If your home is well insulated, you will waste less energy and save yourself money at the same time. It is estimated that as much as 27 per cent of carbon emissions are generated by our own homes, so any improvements you make can have a lasting impact.

- Consider proper loft insulation and cavity-wall insulation.

- Have your central-heating boiler serviced annually.

- Windows are an area of considerable heat loss. Check that they are well-fitting and there are no draughts. Double and triple glazing are preferable, if within your budget.

- Make sure you put weather-proof strips round all your windows if you do not have double-glazing.

- Make sure your hot-water tank and hot-water pipes are properly insulated.

- Check draughts around doors and apply draught-excluder tape if necessary. Curtains across windows or doors will also help to retain heat.

You might like to look into what grants are available in your area for things like cavity-wall insulation, or upgrading your central-heating boiler to a more efficient type. Although this will involve an initial outlay, it should save you money in the long run.

Saving water

Depending on where you live, saving water may be something you think seriously about – or ignore completely because it seems to rain so often! Either way, water is a valuable resource and should be used wisely.

- Fitting a water meter should help you keep a closer eye on your water consumption – which may help you save money.

- Avoid letting the tap run while you are washing up, shaving or cleaning your teeth.

- Only use the washing machine and dishwasher when they have a full load or use a half-load programme if there is one.

- Keep a jug of fresh cold water in the refrigerator rather than running the tap until cold each time you want a drink.

- Have showers rather than baths and cut the time you spend in the shower by a minute or two.

- Don't run more water for the bath than you really need.

- If you have a dual flush on your toilet cistern, use it appropriately. If not, install a Hippo water saver.

- Make sure you fix a leaky tap immediately as dripping taps can waste a lot of water – and be an irritation you could do without.

- Use less hot water by installing low-flow shower heads.

- Teach your children to turn off taps when they have finished at the sink.

- Save your bath water for watering the garden. Water outside in the cool of the morning or evening.

- Install a couple of water butts to collect water from your roof to water your garden.

- If you use a carwash, make sure it is one that recycles its water.

- Use a layer of organic mulch on the soil to minimize water loss.

Sensible shopping

The key to sensible shopping is to do a little organization beforehand. Keep a shopping list on the go somewhere convenient and jot down things as you run out – washing-up liquid, cans of beans, dishwasher tablets, toilet paper and so on.

Plan it, list it, stick to it: Before you go shopping, decide what meals you are going to have for the week and how many people you are serving. Run through your plan and put everything you need on your shopping list, then stick to it.

Special offers: You may well come across offers that change your plans or see some particularly nice fruit or vegetables that you'd like to use – that's fine. But do try to avoid buying the ingredients for the planned dish as well as the replacement one.

Of course, you want to take advantage of offers, but only buy things that you know you will need. If things end up sitting in the kitchen cupboard for a year before being thrown out in your next declutter, that's not a good use of anyone's resources.

Recycled products: Buy recycled paper products, such as stationery, toilet paper and kitchen paper.

A huge amount of food is also thrown away by supermarkets and you may feel that tackling that issue is one you would like to get involved with. Some supermarkets are now baking banana muffins from the bananas that are just beginning to overripen. Others are supplying food that is on its sell-by date to local charities. This is certainly an element in the equation that needs to be addressed.

Old-fashioned thrift

Whether or not you are on a tight budget, making good use of things, avoiding waste and taking care of your property makes sense because it respects your environment and saves you money. One simple way to think about it is to apply the old adage: look after the pennies and the pounds will look after themselves. So use a child's small soft spatula to get every last bit out of the jam or chutney jar; add a little water to the just-about-empty washing-up liquid bottle to eke it out a bit longer, and make food leftovers into other dishes – you will feel the benefit when you do your shopping.

RE-USE

If you look after things, they should last longer and not need replacing. Service appliances regularly to make sure they are working at their best – and repair them quickly if they go wrong. This applies to small items as well as large, and with the smaller ones, you may be able to repair things yourself rather than having to call in an expert. Besides which, small annoyances are disproportionately stressful because they are constantly repeated and difficult to ignore.

Try to buy products that can be used many times, rather than disposable equivalents. Luckily most people are now aware of the huge quantities of plastic carrier bags that were thrown away each year after a single use, and have switched to reusables, but there are other simple changes you can make too. Clingfilm (plastic wrap), for example, can be replaced with stretch-and-stick covers, and baking parchment with silicon moulds or reusable liners. Re-sealable plastic food bags can be used many times, and you can choose reusable plastic containers for freezer food. Consider buying a battery charger and switching to rechargeable batteries too.

Once any item has served its original purpose, perhaps it can be turned into some other useful object. If not, it might be suitable to go to a charity shop to give it the chance to find a new home where it will be useful. Making that small degree of extra effort means as many things as possible will bring pleasure and service to people for longer, rather than just being thrown into landfill.

Upcycle

Many things that have ceased to be useful still have some life in them if you view them with a little imagination.

Bicycle wheels: Half bury them in the ground to make interesting garden-border edges.

Broken bricks: These make good garden edgings too.

CDs: Hang near your seedlings to scare off the birds.

Clothes: Make a child's dress or shorts out of a discarded dress. Try doing some basic patchwork to use up fabric from unwanted clothes or make shopping bags, toy bags or a child's playmat.

Crockery: Use for mosaic.

Duvet: Use the stuffing for toys or cushions.

Fabric: Tear odd pieces of cotton fabric into squares to make cleaning cloths.

Plastic food trays: Wash thoroughly and use to pack items for the freezer, sealing them in plastic bags.

Go online to find more uses for discarded items. If you like to sew, you will find plenty of bloggers who will show you how to reuse just about any fabric.

Make-do activities

There are any number of things that you can make from discarded odds and ends – they'll be fun to make with children and to play with. As well as making good use of unwanted items, the creativity is good for everyone involved because it stimulates the imagination.

Being creative at any level is also good for your well-being. You should enjoy your time messing about with glue and paper, and feel rewarded when you help a child create something they are proud of (or if you create something yourself).

Allocate a box or drawer in which to store a selection of potential craft-project items, so that when you are feeling creative you have a stock of things to inspire your imagination. You could make a miniature puppet theatre, a play shop, birthday cards, skittles, and all sorts of other things. Here are a few things you might save in your drawer:

- cardboard boxes;
- cardboard tubes from kitchen roll;
- cellophane;
- cereal boxes;
- doilies;
- juice containers;
- newspaper;
- plain or coloured paper;
- plastic bottles;
- ribbon;
- scraps of fabric;
- scraps of wrapping paper;
- silver foil;
- socks;
- straws;
- toothpicks (cocktail sticks)
- used matchboxes;
- wallpaper.

You might also collect some craft materials such as:

- buttons and sequins;
- card;
- coloured paper;
- felt-tip pens;
- glue;
- paper clips;
- sticky tape;
- swivel pins.

Birthday cards and pictures: Fold a small piece of card in half and decorate the front with a collage of fancy paper, drawings, sequins and anything else that works.

Fish racing: Cut some fish out of paper about 30cm (12in) long. Mark out a lane for each player and a finishing line and put the fish at the start. Give each player a folded newspaper, which must be flapped in the air behind the fish to propel it down the track as quickly as possible.

Fishing: This is great fun for small children. Take a cardboard shoe box or larger box and have the children paint the inside to look like water. Now get them to draw some fish on pieces of cardboard, paint them with bright colours and cut them out. Slide a paperclip onto the nose of each fish and put them in the pond. Now make some fishing rods out of short pieces of garden cane, sticks or barbecue skewers (take off the sharp point). Attach a piece of string to one end of each rod and then attach a magnet to the other end of the string. The children take turns to see how many fish they can catch on their rods in a given time. To make this game educational, you can paint a number or letter on each fish and get each child to catch the fish in number order, pick up the numbers of their birthday or spell out their name, for example.

Hoopla: Use old plastic drinks bottles and weight them with water, sand or stones. Make hoops out of cardboard, making sure they are large enough

to go over the bottles, and paint them in different colours. See who can throw their hoops over the largest number of bottles.

Jigsaw: Draw a picture or choose one from a magazine and stick it to a piece of card. Draw on jigsaw shapes – of a size to suit the child's ability – then cut them out to make a jigsaw puzzle.

Playing shops: Either use discarded cereal boxes, washed cans and plastic bottles or cut out and decorate smaller items and make your own stuff to fill a play store. Use toy money or buttons as cash.

Puppet theatre: Cut a large opening in the front of a cardboard box that is large enough for two children to fit behind when they perform the show. You will also need to make two holes in the back to allow the children to get their hands through. Get your child to paint some scenery on the inside of the box. Attach a piece of string across the opening at the top, then thread two pieces of fabric along it to make the curtains.

Make some puppets from old brightly coloured socks. Use buttons and thread to make the faces, or paint on the faces using fabric paint. Now ask the children to slip the puppets over their hands and then sit back and enjoy their show.

Shoebox house: Make a house, an office, a garage or shop in an old shoebox. Divide it into different sections with pieces of cardboard and decorate with paint, coloured paper or fabric. Make miniature furniture with old matchboxes, card, paper and used matches or straws.

Skittles: Partially fill old plastic bottles with water to give them some weight. Fix on the lids tightly and line them up to use as skittles to try to knock down with a tennis ball.

Tell-the-time clock: Use a paper plate, a couple of strips of card and a swivel pin to draw and construct a pretend clock to teach a child how to tell the time with an analogue clock.

RECYCLE

Most people now recycle a large proportion of their household waste and this is a vitally important part of making the best use of our natural resources.

Much of it is taken away conveniently every week or fortnight. The method and timings of collections and even which items are collected will vary depending on where you live, so you will need to Google your local council to find out what happens in your area. The collection may include some or all of the following: cans, glass, paper and card, certain plastics, food waste and garden waste. There are many kinds of plastic and only some can be recycled, so make sure you don't put any of the wrong plastic in the collection bin.

The recycling facility

If an item is not collected, then you will need to take it to your local recycling facility. Again, facilities differ so check out the local opportunities.

Separate the things you are taking so they are easy to put into the right places: small or large electrical appliances, books, shoes, clothes, wood, glass, metal, household rubbish, and garden rubbish, for example.

Aerosols: Most recycling facilities will take aerosols provided they are not crushed, pierced or flattened.

Batteries: Most recycling facilities and major supermarkets have a collection bin for batteries and will dispose of them safely for you. (See also Car Batteries, page 42).

Books: Because of the glue in the binding, books cannot be recycled but they are collected and re-used by charities, schools and hospitals so take them to the charity shop or recycling facility.

Building materials: Most building materials, such as bricks and wood, can be reused. Others, such as glass, plastic or metal, can be recycled either at your local depot or at a salvage yard. Commercial waste is chargeds.

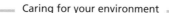

Cans: Cans are usually collected. Rinse them and put them in the box provided.

Car batteries: These must go to the collection point at the recycling facility or local garage.

Cars: The local salvage yard will be able to extract all the recyclable materials.

Clothing: Collection bins are at recycling facilities if that is more convenient than delivering them to a charity shop. Only include good-quality items that can be re-sold.

Computers, cameras and electrical goods: Some charities will collect or accept donations of working televisions, computers, cameras, and so on. Otherwise, dispose of them at the recycling facility.

Glass: Sort glass into green, brown and clear. Some banks can recycle screw tops so you can leave them on the bottles.

Metal: Any metal, apart from cans, should go to the designated area at the local recycling facility.

Mobile phones: Your phone supplier, various charities or local supermarkets may have a scheme for refurbishing old phones or recycling the parts.

Paint: Seal cans well to stop them drying out, then take them to your local recycling facility where you'll find a donation point. Paint is usually given to a local community repainting scheme.

Paper: All kinds of paper can be recycled and it is often divided into separate categories: newspapers, magazines, cardboard, office paper, and so on. Even phone books can be recycled these days. Avoid shredding paper unless it contains private details, as many authorities are unable to take it in this form and many of the processing plants are unable to handle shredded paper.

Plastic: There are over 50 different types of plastic and almost all of these can be accepted by recycling facilities. Make sure any plastic bottles are washed clean and preferably pressed flat. Rinsing them in boiling water will make that easier.

Printer cartridges: Some charities and schools used to collect these for recycling but it is no longer cost-effective for most cartridges. However, it is worth checking, perhaps online, whether your particular cartridges can be donated to someone.

Spectacles: Leave your unwanted spectacles with your optician as they will have a scheme for donating them to those less fortunate.

Caring for yourself and others

Staying healthy and happy

If you respect your environment, then it stands to reason that you must also respect yourself, and that means taking care of your health and well-being, so this chapter will give you some hints and tips on staying healthy and looking after yourself.

Prevention is always better than cure, so if you follow a healthy, balanced diet, take regular exercise and avoid excesses, you are doing all you can to ensure that your body functions at its best. You wouldn't put lemonade in a Porsche and expect it to perform. Similarly, you need to put the right type and quality of food into your body to make it perform, and to drink plenty of water to keep the system functioning efficiently. In this chapter, we are going to look at the broader picture of how to look after yourself – and pamper yourself, too – then in the next chapter, we'll go into more detail on diet.

EXERCISE

Taking exercise is not just about using up calories. It is about keeping our metabolism working, and our joints and muscles supple, strengthening the heart, getting plenty of fresh air, improving breathing and releasing the endorphins that help to make us feel good.

The first important point is that you should not be forcing yourself to go to the gym or go running if you hate it. It won't last and you'll just end up thinking all exercise is equally boring and give up. You need to find something you like – that's really all that matters. So look into what's available locally and what your friends enjoy, get ideas from anywhere you can and see if you can organize a taster session, or go along to see if it's up your street. If you are not sure – or even if you think you are but have the opportunity to try something – try it. You never know what will interest and excite you.

One of the best things to do is to incorporate physical activity, especially a brisk walk, into your daily routine, so that may be a good starting point to get you going. Just implementing these few little changes can make a big difference:

- Get off the bus a stop early and walk the rest of the way.

- Don't take the lift or the escalator, take the stairs.

- Leave the car at home, especially for any distances of less than 2–3km (1¼–1¾ miles).

- Offer to walk a neighbour's dog once or twice a week – or walk your own.

- Think about indoor exercise (at home or at a class): Pilates, yoga, bodypump or aerobics, for example.

- Consider team games: football, rugby, netball, basketball.

- Do you fancy watersports: rowing, sailing, swimming?

- What about indoor sports: table tennis, badminton, squash?

AVOIDING SICKNESS

You can't completely avoid coming into contact with germs and diseases, but there are some things you can do to reduce the chances of catching anything, in particular the coughs and colds that can spread so rapidly.

Avoid close contact

If you have a nasty cold and are sneezing, coughing or blowing your nose all the time, then you are likely to be spreading your germs to anyone close to you. They won't thank you for it. If you are well enough to work, you may have a job that allows you to work from home for a day; many companies are becoming more flexible on this score. When you cough or sneeze, try to do it into a tissue, then dispose of it. Sensible colleagues will extend the same courtesy.

Boost your immune system

A regular dose of echinacea, following the manufacturer's recommendations, should boost your immune system and help you fight off infections.

To start the day, sip a drink made from a squeezed lemon and boiling water. It cleanses the liver, gets your metabolism off to a flying start and is a great source of vitamin C. And if you want to give it some extra zest, try adding some chopped ginger root.

Detox

At its most extreme, detoxing can mean drinking nothing but water and carrot juice for a week, but that's not a common-sense approach. Instead, try to have one day a week when you eat nothing but beautifully fresh, organic vegetables and drink nothing but water and you will find that the boost to your system is out of all proportion to the effort involved.

Regular check-ups

If you have regular appointments with your doctor or dentist, do make sure you attend. They may be able to pick up and deal with an incipient issue before it becomes more serious. If you are experiencing unexplained problems, make notes of the symptoms. It is more efficient than relying on your memory and the doctor will be better placed to make a diagnosis the more information he or she has.

BEAUTY TIPS AND HOMEMADE COSMETICS

Whether or not you wear make-up, it is good to take care of your skin, and men are now realizing that this applies just as much to them as to women. It is fun to make natural skin-care treatments and cosmetics from natural ingredients. Just remember that they must be treated as fresh products as they contain no preservatives.

This is not just about vanity. Looking after your skin will not only help you look better but you'll feel better too. Taking time out to treat yourself is a great way of relaxing and de-stressing, so get out those scented candles, fill a hot bath and indulge in some of these beauty tips and treats every now and again.

Bath time

Milk bath: Add three or four tablespoons of dried milk powder to your bathwater – it's much cheaper than using lots of milk.

Oat bath: Put some oats in an old stocking, tie a knot in it and put it in the bath. The oats turn the water milky and moisturize your skin beautifully.

Cosmetics

Eyeliner: If your eyeliner is always smudging, try dipping a wet brush in dark eye shadow and using that instead.

Face powder: Loose powder sticks to moisturizers and cleansers and can look very heavy. Avoid this by blotting your face with a tissue before you put on any powder.

Always store your powder puff face towards the mirror in your compact as residual oil from your skin can affect the powder in your compact.

Foundation: Using a foundation brush or tapping your foundation onto your face rather than blending it in gives much better coverage.

Don't use the same foundation all year round. In summer, you may need a slightly darker tone but lighter texture. Don't automatically buy the same shade when you replace your foundation as skin changes over time.

For that special, smooth summer look, mix a little moisturizer into your foundation before applying it.

Foundation for a florid complexion: If you have a reddish complexion, use a foundation with a greenish tinge, or use a green-tinted moisturizer underneath to neutralize the colour.

Shiny face: If you know you tend to get a shiny face when warm, do make sure you use a good primer (even if you don't use foundation).

Unruly eyebrows: If, even after you have plucked them, your eyebrows are still all over the place, apply a little styling gel or mousse with an eyebrow brush to smooth and shape them.

Eye bags

Many people trust to holding an ice cube under each eye until the cube melts. The Hollywood solution is to gently rub some haemorrhoid cream into the offending area.

The morning after a big night out, dab a very small blob of eye gel around the eye, especially underneath, as soon as you have washed your face. Leave it for a little while before using your usual moisturizer and then applying some concealer.

Eyelashes

If you don't like wearing mascara or are sensitive to it, ask your beautician (or hairdresser) to dye your eyelashes with a mild, vegetable dye. It will keep your lashes dark and lustrous for up to two months – and if you like the effect, have it done again.

Freshening up

To keep your make-up looking as if it has just been applied, no matter how hot you feel, keep a small spray of water in your bag and give your face a light spray every so often.

Foot care

Give your feet a treat every week by indulging in a footbath. Pour some warm water into a suitable-size basin, then sprinkle in some bath salts and a few drops of lavender or another favourite essential oil. Soak your feet for 15 minutes, treat them with an exfoliator to get rid of hard skin, dry them with a thick, clean towel and rub in a little foot lotion.

Another solution for hard skin is to soak in ½ cup of mouthwash, ½ cup of vinegar and 1 cup of warm water, the scrub and moisturize with a few drops of peppermint essential oil in some sweet almond oil.

Hair care

Shampoo: Ignore the advice on shampoo bottles to shampoo your hair twice – it is not necessary, especially if you shampoo every day or so. If you shampoo too often, you are in danger of stripping your hair of natural oils.

Shining hair: For soft, shining hair, use cold water for the final rinse and let your hair dry naturally, under a towel wrapped around your head. And when you come to brush it out, wrap a silk scarf round your hairbrush and use it to brush your hair.

Tangled hair: If you have long hair that gets tangled when you wash it, start brushing at the ends first, working your way back towards the scalp.

Hand cream
If you are out of hand cream, mix a teaspoon of sugar with a teaspoon of olive oil, rub it into your hands, then wash your hands.

Lip care
Applying lipstick: If you smooth a little foundation and a touch of translucent powder onto your lips before you put your lipstick on, it will last a lot longer.

Broken lipstick: If your favourite lipstick breaks, you can carefully repair it by melting the broken edges with a lighted match then gently pressing the pieces back together. Use a toothpick to smooth the edges, then keep the lipstick in the refrigerator for a couple of hours to set.

Lip brush: You will get a more professional finish by using a lip brush.

Lip liner: Using a lip liner in an identical shade to your lipstick will give you a professional finish. If you put your lip liner – cap on – in a glass of warm water for five minutes before applying it, it will go on smoothly.

Nail care
Base layer: Use a colourless base layer to stops nails discolouring.

Dirty nails: If you have been gardening or doing other messy jobs and your nails are dirty, rub your fingertips across a piece of soft soap so the soap goes behind your nails. Wash your hands, then rinse under hot running water and the soap will wash out the dirt.

Drying varnish: If you are in a rush to go out and your nail varnish hasn't dried, as long as it has been on for 20 minutes, you can run your nails under cold water to speed up the process.

Preparing nails for varnish: Dark varnish and some fast-drying varnishes can make nails go yellow. To prevent this happening, rub in some almond oil, give the nails a good buffing until they glow like pearls and give them a break from the nail varnish for a day or two.

Rolled not shaken: If your nail varnish bubbles, try rolling the bottle gently to even out the colour, rather than shaking it.

Short nails: To make nails look longer, go for darker shades and don't paint the nails quite to the sides.

Splitting nails: Rubbing your nails with warm olive oil moisturizes them, softens the cuticles and helps them splitting.

Storing varnish: Nail varnish stays fresher for longer if you keep it in the refrigerator.
   If you find that the top of your varnish bottle is always sticking, rub a little petroleum jelly inside the top of the bottle.

Tanned hands: If you want to make your hands look more tanned, use a very pale purply-pink nail varnish.

Toenails: Painted toenails look great with sandals and flip-flops; painted toes don't. Avoid getting paint on your toes by twisting a tissue into a long piece and feeding it backwards and forwards between your toes to keep them separate.

Whitening nails: If the tips of your nails are yellow or cream and you want them white, cut a lemon in half and push your nails into the flesh for a few minutes.

Perfume

Applying perfume: You know, of course, to apply perfume behind your ears, at the temples and the nape of the neck, at the crook of the elbow and inside the wrists, but in summer when you are not wearing tights, try dabbing just a little behind the knees. Perfume rises and just a little at the pulse points works wonders.

Buying perfume: The initial aroma, or top notes, of a perfume dry down to the middle notes and then to the base notes, which is the scent that lingers. Apply the tester, then return to the shop after an hour or two if you still like the fragrance.

Fragrant hair: Spray a little perfume onto your hairbrush before you brush your hair to spread a gentle fragrance.

Fragrant body: Spray a cloud of your favourite *eau de toilette* into the air after you have dressed for the day, walk into it and you will smell beautifully for hours.

Perfume strengths: The cost of perfume reflects the concentration. *Parfum* is highly concentrated so you need less, *eau de parfum* comes next, followed by *eau de toilette*.

Sunny days: Avoid wearing perfume in the sun. Many contain oils that might cause brown spots on the skin.

Skin care

Everyone – men and women – should cleanse and moisturize their face each day for radiant skin. When you apply moisturizer, avoid the eye area – the skin there is very delicate. Also the moisturizer tends to coat the eyelashes, which makes mascara run.

You can make expensive body lotions last twice as long by mixing them half-and-half with inexpensive, unperfumed body lotion. You won't notice any reduction in the strength of the scent and you'll save money, too.

After-bath body moisturizer: Mix two tablespoons of almond oil with a few drops of lavender essential oil to moisturize dry skin and reduce scarring.

Cleanser: Mix equal quantities of buttermilk, plain yogurt and cream to cleanse and plump the skin.
    Add two to three drops of sandalwood or lavender oil to two tablespoons of milk and massage gently all over the face.

Exfoliator: Mix granulated sugar and water to a paste, rub gently over the face, then rinse off.

Exfoliator for greasy skin: Mix a tablespoon of ground rice with a tablespoon of cornflour (corn starch) and a few drops of lemon juice. Rub gently over the face, leave for 20 minutes, then rinse off.

Exfoliator for sensitive skin: Make a paste of honey and oats, spread on the face and leave for 20 minutes, then rinse off.

Face pack (banana): Mash a banana and spread it over the face. Leave for 20 minutes, then rinse off with warm water.

Face pack (egg): Beat an egg yolk and mix with a teaspoon of orange juice, a teaspoon of rosewater and a few drops of lime juice. Rub gently over the face and leave for 20 minutes, then rinse off with warm water.

Face pack for greasy skin: Spread honey over your face and leave for 20 minutes, then rinse off to cleanse and moisturize the skin.

Moisturizer for dry skin: If you have dry skin, massage the face and body lightly with almond oil or olive oil every night before going to bed.

Toner for greasy skin: Dab your face with aloe vera gel and allow to dry. This will get rid of dead skin cells and tone and moisturize your skin.

SIMPLE HEALTH REMEDIES

Minor health issues often have simple solutions based on natural substances. This section gives you information on all kinds of remedies for common problems. Remember that you should always consult your doctor about any health issues that concern you, and take advantage of any health screening for early detection of serious problems.

Acne

If your adolescent children are having problems with acne, add two tablespoons of white vinegar to a cup of cooled, boiled water. Tell them to wash the face thoroughly and then apply the solution to the affected area. Don't expect a flawless complexion overnight, but after a week you should see a big improvement. Make sure the youngsters are following a healthy diet and drinking plenty of water.

Ageing

There's nothing you can do about growing older but if you want to grow old healthily (forget the gracefully), then you need to take care of yourself. The best way to do that is to maintain a healthy diet and take regular exercise. Try to maintain your interests (or even take up new ones) to keep your mind stimulated and make every effort not to become isolated – companionship is very important at any stage of life. Introduce yourself to your neighbours, go to a church or a social club, take up a new hobby or maintain an old one. Learn to use a computer.

The metabolism slows down as you age, and joints and muscles tend to become less responsive. It is generally best to keep moving – use it or lose it. However, there may come a time when mobility aids are necessary, in which case, look on the internet, find a local mobility-aid supplier or talk to your doctor; there may well be gadgets that make light work of tasks you are now finding difficult.

Prostate problems: Prostate cancer most commonly (but not exclusively) affects older men. The statistics prove that early intervention leads to excellent outcomes, so men should not hesitate to be checked by their doctor. Normally the size of a walnut, the prostate can become enlarged, which can cause uncomfortable urinary problems.

One of the best natural remedies for prostate problems is to eat pumpkin seeds as they are a rich source of unsaturated fatty acid. This is vital to the health of the prostate, so eat 55g (2oz) daily either as a snack or cooked in food.

Anxiety

Lavender is a very calming herb that can be useful to relax you if you suffer from anxiety. Use a scented candle or diffuser in your room; immerse a handful of flowers in 600ml (1 pint/2½ cups) of cider vinegar and take a few deep breaths of the fragrance; or sprinkle a few drops of lavender essential oil on a clean handkerchief and breath it in.

Try taking a dessertspoon of ginseng elixir before you have breakfast and drink ginseng tea rather than your usual brew. During the day, sip a glass of hot water with a teaspoon of honey.

Steam a large handful of nettle tops until they are tender, add two teaspoons of honey and eat as a vegetable with your main meal of the day. Don't worry about stinging your mouth – the cooking takes the sting out of the nettle.

Athlete's foot

If you tend to suffer from this fungal infection, make sure you are scrupulous about drying between your toes and perhaps use a little talcum powder after drying to reduce your chances of reinfection.

Rinse your feet several times a day with cider vinegar to get rid of the infection. Always put on clean tights or socks after doing this and soak old ones in a solution of one part vinegar to five parts water before washing them.

The condition can often be cured by treating with a few drops of tea-tree oil diluted in a few tablespoons of a carrier oil, such as sweet almond oil, rubbed into the toes.

Bedwetting

If your toddler is out of nappies but is not reliably dry at night, try not giving him or her anything to drink for three hours before going to bed. A traditional remedy to help toddlers stay dry overnight is to give them a tablespoonful of honey just before you clean their teeth.

Bites and stings

Bee stings: Remove the sting if it has been left behind in the skin as quickly as possible because it will continue to pump out toxin. Use tweezers gently or flick out the sting with the point of a knife – whatever you do, don't squeeze it in the process. Dilute some bicarbonate of soda (baking soda) in water and rub over the area. Tea tree oil can also help. If the stinger has been left behind, you have been stung by a honey bee. This bee (which will now die) will have given off an alarm pheromone because it saw you as a threat. This pheromone is a call to arms, so it is best to move on quickly.

Mosquito bites: You can buy a small device in major chemists that you touch on a bite, preferably as soon as possible, and give yourself a small electric shock. This can stop the bite from developing.

Nettle stings: Rub with a dock leaf or lavender oil.

Relief from stings and bites: Apart from over-the-counter remedies, you can use vinegar, tea-tree essential oil, lavender essential oil, aloe vera gel or witch hazel liquid, a fresh, cut onion or toothpaste to dab on the sting.

Repellents: Since it's better not to get bitten in the first place, use a good-quality repellent. You could also try rubbing lavender oil on your skin, or a 50:50 mixture of vanilla extract and water. Some people take vitamin B1, or thiamine, tablets. By taking twice the recommended daily allowance, the excess of this water-soluble vitamin is excreted through the skin, which apparently deters the mosquitoes. Eating lots of garlic can also put off stinging insects because the smell permeates the skin. Unfortunately, it can also put off the people around you!

Burning candles, especially citronella, deters insects, as does a pot of growing basil on the windowsill.

Wasp stings: Rub the affected area with either lemon juice or vinegar.

When more is needed: If you know yourself to be allergic to the stings of any insect, if a bite feels more painful or swells more than expected, or if you have been bitten and now feel flu-like, you should take an antihistamine tablet and consider whether to take further action. If your breathing starts to feel laboured, call for an ambulance at once.

Blisters
Don't break the blister. Wash the skin with clean water and gently pat dry. Mix some lavender or tea-tree oil into a suitable vegetable oil such as olive, almond or sesame – one part lavender or tea tree to five parts vegetable oil. Apply to the blister and allow it to soak in.

If you have some chamomile tea bags, simply moisten one and hold it on the blister. Or apply an infusion of St John's wort, using a clean piece of cotton wool, several times a day.

The blues
Everyone feels down from time to time, lacking in energy, prone to tears and generally low. With a little help, you can usually pull yourself back to normal with a few sensible remedies but do not hesitate to contact your doctor if you feel it is going on too long or you are losing control of your life. Depression is a serious issue and is much better dealt with in the early stages. Here, we are talking about beating the blues rather than coping with depression.

If you know why you are feeling down, that's a great help as you may be able to deal with the issues that are causing the problem. Ideally you should address them as soon as you can because the longer you leave them, the more the stress can build. Some things, such as grief for the loss of a loved one, you know you will have to endure for a time, but you can still work slowly towards coming to terms with what has happened. Here are a few tips to help you along the way:

- Don't be too tough on yourself. Allow yourself time to grieve by factoring in plenty of rest time. Don't fill up your diary with too many things. You will use a lot of emotional energy when you are feeling blue and that will mean you will have less physical energy.

- Try not to indulge your feelings all the time. Allow yourself time to think about the sadness but introduce small distractions and let yourself enjoy them – they can help take your mind off your problem. Spending time outside often helps too.

- Plenty of sleep is important. Make sure your bedroom is relaxing, add a lavender diffuser or a few drops of lavender oil on the pillow and perhaps listen to some soft music. Relax in a warm bath with a few drops of lavender oil. Sit in bed with a warm, milky drink or a cup of chamomile tea. Consider taking a herbal sleeping tablet if necessary.

- You may find your appetite is reduced but try to eat healthily and regularly in small quantities until you feel better.

Bruises

Use an ice-cold compress, or a bag of frozen peas wrapped in a cloth, and apply to the bruise for up to ten minutes. Put a few drops of lavender oil on the cloth if you have some.

Arnica is a well-known remedy for bruises. Apply as a cream as long as the skin is not broken. You can also buy it as ampoules.

Witch hazel is another useful herb to combat bruising. Make up some ice cubes containing crushed witch hazel, or freeze liquid witch hazel, and keep them handy to place on top of a bruised area.

Burns (minor)

Run a burn under cool water for at least ten minutes. If the burn is larger than the patient's hand, on the face, hands or feet, or is deep, call for medical help. Remove any jewellery or clothing near the burn, unless it is stuck. Cover with cling film (plastic wrap) or a clean plastic bag. If necessary, treat for shock (see page 74). For minor burns and where the skin is not broken, apply one of the following:

- Aloe vera – a cool and soothing gel that has been used for thousands of years to treat minor burns.

- Lavender oil, which has strong antiseptic properties and can help heal burns. If applied quickly, it can help prevent scarring.

- Arnica, which may help take the sting out of minor burns. Taken in tablet form, it can help with shock and trauma.

Cold sores

As soon as you feel that slight tingle on your lips that heralds a cold sore, swamp a piece of gauze with witch hazel and dab it on the area. It often stops the sore developing, but if you are too late, repeat the witch hazel treatment, ignore the sting and the sore will soon dry out. Diluted white vinegar works for some, too.

Constipation

Avoidance is better than dealing with constipation, so include plenty of fibre in your diet, stay active and drink sufficient water. If you do become constipated, try increasing your liquid intake and eating figs, prunes, oranges, All Bran or liquorice, or you can drink chicory (endive) coffee. A natural solution is preferable to taking laxatives on a regular basis.

Corns

Mix a teaspoonful of wholemeal flour and a drizzle of vinegar to make a paste, adding a little more flour to get a decent consistency. Spread this over the corn and press a thin slice of onion over it. Wrap a bandage round to keep everything in place and leave it overnight.

Coughs and colds

It is virtually impossible to avoid catching a cold from time to time but the antibacterial properties in garlic can help the immune system fight off infection, so include it in your cooking. Here are a few tips to help ease potential symptoms:

Blocked-up nose: Fill a hot-water bottle with really hot (but not boiling) water, add several drops of eucalyptus or camphor oil and tightly stopper it. When your nose bungs up, simply unscrew the stopper and inhale.

Menthol crystals are available from the pharmacy. Put a few in an egg cup, add a few drops of boiling water and inhale.

Catarrh: Clear catarrh from the head and sinuses by breathing in the fumes from a few drops of eucalyptus essential oil on a handkerchief at regular intervals.

Chesty coughs: Put a sliced lemon and three cups of water in a saucepan and bring to the boil. Add two tablespoons of honey and two of glycerine. Stir well, remove the lemon and sip the elixir throughout the day.

Headache: Make a soothing drink of honey and lemon in hot water, or try a sage tea.

High temperature: Oranges, lemons and grapefruit all have healing properties. Orange and grapefruit can bring down a temperature and lemon helps to cleanse and purify the system.

Sore throat: Take an eggcup of water, add two or three drops of lavender essential oil and a teaspoonful of vodka, gargle and spit out. This should ease a sore throat.

Tickly cough: A spoonful of honey can help soothe a sore throat and banish the irritation of a tickly cough. A drink of honey and lemon in hot water is also soothing.

Cramp

If you suffer from cramp in the feet or legs at night, try avoiding or limiting alcohol before you go to bed. During the day, drink plenty of water and other liquids; your urine should be pale yellow. Eat foods that are rich in calcium, potassium and magnesium, such as fish, leafy green vegetables, bananas, yogurt and dark chocolate. Eating a banana or a square of dark chocolate before you go to bed may help.

Avoid cold feet, so try wearing a pair of loose bedrocks or using a heated oat bag or hot water bottle. A syrup made up of a teaspoonful each of honey, cider vinegar and calcium lactate (available online) is often said to keep cramp at bay.

When cramp strikes, stretching and movement can help. You can also try pinching your top lip and squeezing hard until the cramp dies down.

Cuts and grazes

Tea-tree oil has both antiseptic and antifungal properties which make it ideal for treating minor cuts and grazes.

Warm extra-virgin olive oil can be applied directly to damaged skin. The astringent and antiseptic qualities in olives help to clean and protect the wound from infection.

Soak four teaspoons of red clover flowers in 600ml (1 pint/2½ cups) of hot water for ten minutes. Allow it to cool and then soak some cotton wool in the liquid and apply directly to the wound.

Boil a handful of lavender flowers in 600ml (1 pint/2½ cups) of water, allow the mixture to cool and then strain and dab onto the skin using clean cotton wool.

Diarrhoea

This can be a symptom of a number of conditions, so do not delay contacting your doctor if you are concerned. In the first instance, stop eating for 24 hours and drink plenty of water and flat Coca-Cola or lemonade, sipping it gradually throughout the day. If that improves the situation, start eating toast or rice in small quantities, still taking plenty of liquids, until you feel better. Ginger tea can ease any discomfort.

For babies and young children, you should seek professional advice immediately.

Dry hands

Remember to apply hand cream generously before you go to bed every night, then regularly during the day.

Eye care

One of the most popular treatments to soothe tired eyes is to put moistened chamomile teabags on closed eyelids and then relax for ten minutes.

If you spend hour after hour at the computer staring at the screen, buy the best pair of lightly tinted sunglasses you can afford and wear them from time to time when you are working. And if you wear glasses, ask your optician about a prescription for a pair of glasses with a hint of a tint – it's amazing how quickly your eyes will feel the benefit.

Hangover

If you remind yourself how lousy you felt the last time you had a hangover, use that thought to remind you to alternate a glass of wine, or whatever alcohol you are drinking, with a glass of water if you know you are in for a heavy night. Even if you do feel bad in the morning, it'll be a lot better than it could have been.

Remember that you almost certainly have a lot of alcohol still in your bloodstream in the morning so you should not attempt to drive.

Sleep as long as you can to let your body recover. Keep some water or orange juice by the bed and have a drink if you wake up. Then try some of these remedies and see which one has the most positive effect for you.

- Try a banana for breakfast. They are high in potassium and can help to balance the body salts.

- Take two tablespoons of honey every few hours until you feel better.

- Have a cup of sweet dandelion tea, or introduce dandelion leaves into a salad, if you are up to that kind of food (dandelion leaves are very bitter). Dandelion also restores the body's potassium and helps eliminate the toxins caused by drinking. But don't take in too much dandelion because it is also a diuretic.

- Chamomile tea is a general soother and helps your body to relax. It works wonders on the hangover headache and helps to settle the stomach, especially when sweetened with honey.

- Lemon and lime are two of nature's refreshers, so a glass of cool water mixed with the juice of either of these will act as a pick-me-up.

- Make an infusion using mint or chew on a fresh leaf to calm the stomach, freshen your stale breath and ease a headache.

- Drink a lukewarm cup of fennel tea to help overcome nausea.

- Rosemary is a natural stimulant. Either use it in the bath or chop some over a salad to relieve feelings of tiredness.

Hay fever and other allergies

Allergies are becoming increasingly common and can have complex symptoms and causes. You should always consult with your doctor or specialist about your specific problems but there are things you can try that should have some benefits without risk of side-effects. If you can work out what you are allergic to, it can help you deal with the condition by avoiding the specific allergen as far as possible and by being prepared. For example, if you are allergic to grass pollen, you will be affected in different circumstances from someone allergic to tree pollen. Here are some tips to help.

- Keep a diary of your symptoms and try to find the common factors to identify the allergen.

- Find a source of local honey by researching local beekeeping societies on the internet and buy some honey produced as near to your home as possible. Take a teaspoonful every day – throughout the year – and it should reduce your hay fever reactions.

- The boost a daily echinacea tablet gives to the immune system can also help the body deal with hay fever.

- Add garlic to your diet a month or two before the hay fever season begins – it helps boost your immune system, making you more resistant to allergens.

- Chamomile can help soothe red and itchy eyes. Make a weak cup of chamomile tea, allow to cool and then soak a couple of cotton-wool pads in the solution. Gently place over the eyes and leave until the soreness has subsided.

- A herbal infusion of elderflowers is both an excellent preventative measure and treatment for hay fever.

- Nettles are full of chlorophyll and formic acid, both of which help to strengthen the immune system against hay fever. They can either be made into a tea or eaten as a spring vegetable.

- Throw out air fresheners, as they can cause allergic reactions.

- Use non-biological washing solutions.

- Switch to bedding with non-allergenic fillings. If you are allergic to dust mites, buy special mite-proof cases for your mattress and pillows and wash your bed linen frequently.

Headaches

Headaches can have many causes and should not be ignored. If the pain is associated with a head trauma of any kind, consult a doctor.

Here are some old-fashioned remedies for relieving simple or tension headaches.

- Try a cold flannel on your forehead; lie down and relax with the flannel in place because the headache could be caused by tension. Learning to meditate can help you relax (see page 28).

- See if you can find someone to give you a neck massage or do it yourself.

- Make a small muslin bag and fill it with dried marjoram, rosemary and mint. Whenever you feel a headache coming on, hold this scented sachet up to your nose and inhale deeply until you feel the pain subsiding.

- Drink an infusion of a teaspoon each of crushed rosemary leaves and crushed sage leaves in a cup of boiling water. Cover the cup and allow to steep until the tea reaches room temperature. Strain and drink in half-cup doses twice times a day.

- Make a compress by putting five drops of lavender essential oil in cold water. Soak a soft cloth and put it on your forehead.

- Mix a few drops of peppermint oil into a tablespoon of almond oil or other carrier oil and rub on your temples to try to ease a tension headache. Do not use peppermint oil neat, and do not use it on children or on anyone with sensitive skin as it can have an irritant effect.

If you frequently suffer from severe headaches, make sure you take a trip to the doctor because it might be the symptom of a more serious problem.

Head lice

Head lice spread quickly by crawling from head to head and laying their eggs. They are not a sign of bad hygiene – they like clean hair best. They can sometimes be deterred during a school epidemic by applying lavender essential oil to the child's hairline, behind the ears and at the nape of the neck, and by regular brushing. However, if one person in the group is not dealing with the problem, it may recur, in which case there are many proprietary lotions that combat the problem; you should use the one recommended.

Herbs

This quick reference includes the traditional uses of most popular herbs.

Aloe vera	Healing and soothing, particularly for minor burns and skin irritation.
Angelica	Aids digestion and helps dispel uncomfortable stomach cramps and flatulence.
Arnica	Reduces pain, swelling and bruising.
Calendula	Helps balance oestrogen levels and promotes healing.
Celery	Has anti-inflammatory properties and can reduce water retention.
Chamomile	Soothing sedative.
Chicory (endive)	Acts as a laxative and digestive aid and can reduce water retention.
Chilli/cayenne	Acts as an expectorant, decongestant, analgesic, anti-inflammatory and anticoagulant and can lower cholesterol.
Dandelion	A diuretic, used to reduce water retention.

Echinacea	Helps boost the body's immune system and therefore its ability to heal.
Fennel	Antispasmodic and helps increase milk flow in nursing mothers.
Feverfew	Reduces inflammation, helps to improve circulation and can also be beneficial in the treatment of migraines.
Garlic	Helps fight off infection and is beneficial in cardiovascular treatments.
Ginger	Eases pain from flatulence and diarrhoea, aids digestion and helps ease motion sickness.
Lavender	Great at lifting spirits, helps in relaxation and settles the stomach during stress.
Lemon balm	Aids digestion, helps stop stomach cramps and is antiviral.
Liquorice root	Acts as an expectorant and also has antiviral and anti-inflammatory properties.
Mint	Aids digestion, reduces flatulence and helps alleviate nausea.
Nasturtium	Good source of vitamin C and helps build up a resistance to infection.
Plantain	Helps to reduce catarrh and can also be applied topically to stop bleeding in minor cuts and to soothe nettle stings.
Raspberry leaf	Can help to ease menstrual pains.
Rosemary	Improves blood supply to the head.
Sage	Helps reduce inflammation in mucous membranes and aids digestion.
St John's wort	Helps with mild depression.
Thyme	A good expectorant and also has antibacterial and antifungal properties.
Turmeric	Anti-inflammatory and a powerful antioxidant.
Witch hazel	Anti-inflammatory and soothes sunburn and skin irritations.

Hot flushes

Keep a cold pack or a wine-cooler tube in the freezer. When you have a hot flush, slide the wine cooler onto your wrist and hold there wherever the veins are prominent to cool yourself down.

Insomnia

If you are finding it hard to sleep, place a pot-pourri of dried herbs – lime blossom, hops, rosemary, lavender, jasmine and chamomile – in a flat linen 'envelope' and tuck it inside your pillow. The herbs, particularly the hops and lime blossom, have strong sleep-inducing properties. A gentle lavender fragrance can also help; try a lavender reed diffuser in the room or apply a few drops of essential oil to your pillow.

Avoid any stimulation when you are trying to sleep: noise, television, or other interference. Make sure you are comfortable and warm. Then run through the relaxation and meditation techniques (see page 28) to help you relax.

Jet lag

As soon as you get on the plane, set your watch to the time zone of your destination and use that timing straight away so your body's rhythms adapt to the new pattern. Drink plenty of water to stay well hydrated. Avoid alcohol and caffeine, both of which are dehydrating. Eat light, nutritious meals, timed according to your destination time zone. Get up and walk around occasionally and try to get some fresh air when you arrive.

Motion sickness

In general, keep your head still and try to close your eyes and sleep or, at least, rest. Fresh air is beneficial. Avoid reading or watching moving objects. Try ginger or mint tea to help soothe the nausea, or chamomile tea to soothe the nerves.

Many people find that watching the road ahead helps with car sickness, while watching the horizon helps with seasickness.

Nausea

If you are experiencing nausea, especially with a headache, try drinking a glass of pure peach juice to settle your stomach. Alternatively, add half a teaspoon of ground ginger to a cup of boiling water and allow to stand for three minutes before drinking.

Nosebleed

Sit quietly with your head upright or slightly forward (not tilted back) so any blood drains out of the nostrils. Pinch the soft part of the nose, pausing every ten minutes, until the nosebleed stops. Make sure you breathe through the mouth and try to avoid coughing, spitting or sniffing, as this may break blood clots that are forming.

An icepack applied to the bridge of the nose can help stem the bleeding, as can a wet towel placed on the head. As with any bleeding, if it is profuse and does not appear to be stopping, you should call for medical help.

Skin rashes, itching and irritation

Skin allergies can be caused by a vast number of things so it is helpful if you can identify and avoid the problem. Do not use any cosmetic products on the affected area and do not wear jewellery, especially any that contains nickel.

The following remedies may help to relieve minor irritation.

Aloe vera: Slice off a portion of the leaf and apply the gel directly to the affected area (or use a tube of aloe vera gel from the pharmacy).

Bicarbonate of soda (baking soda): A few spoonfuls in a warm bath is good to ease the itching of chicken pox or skin irritations.

Calendula: The oil is often used to reduce the inflammation of nappy rash. You can use the actual herb by putting two teaspoons of calendula in 225ml (8fl oz/1 cup) of boiling water. Leave it to simmer for about ten minutes, then strain and leave to cool. Apply to the affected area.

Oats: Pour some boiling water over a bowl of rolled oats. Cover the bowl and leave to soak for ten minutes. Strain the water and pour it into an ice-cube tray. Freeze and use the ice cubes to relieve the itching by gently rubbing them over the affected area.

Witch hazel: Apply witch hazel gel, or simmer 30g (1oz) fresh witch hazel bark in 600ml (1 pint/2½ cups) of water and leave for ten minutes, then strain and leave to cool. Apply with clean cotton wool and leave it on the skin for 30 minutes.

Spots and blemishes

Dab a little mudpack on a pimple or other occasional skin blemish before going to bed at night. By morning, the impurities should have been drawn out and you should be spot-free.

Stomach upsets and indigestion

Stomach cramps can be caused by a lack of fibre in the diet, so make sure you get plenty of fibre by regularly eating an apple and a banana, and include other fibre-rich foods in your diet, such as oats, beans and lentils. Here are some other things that might help:

Caraway: Place a teaspoon of caraway seeds in a cup and add boiling water. Allow it to stand for ten minutes, strain well and drink up to three cups a day on an empty stomach. Alternatively, you can simply chew on a few caraway seeds after dinner to help stave off indigestion.

Cardamom: Deseed a cardamom pod and chew the seeds with a large glass of water.

Cinnamon: Great at stimulating the digestive system; make a pleasant tea by stirring ½ teaspoon of ground cinnamon into a cup of hot water. Allow to stand for five minutes before drinking.

Fennel: A wonderful herb for calming gas and stomach cramps; make a tea using a teaspoon of fennel seeds to a cup of boiling water. Allow to stand for ten minutes and then strain before drinking on an empty stomach.

Honey and vinegar: Make a syrup of a tablespoonful each of honey and vinegar, then take by the teaspoon when necessary, followed by a glass of water.

Ginger: This has been used for centuries to help stomach ailments of all types, particularly nausea. Add half a teaspoon of ground ginger to a cup of boiling water and allow to stand for three minutes before drinking.

Mint: Many proprietary medicines for upset stomach are flavoured with mint, and this is because mint helps food move through the intestines properly. Make a mint tea by putting a sprig of mint in a cup and adding boiling water. Leave to infuse for ten minutes, strain and drink, preferably on an empty stomach.

Stress

Stress affects both your mind and your body and, if allowed to continue over long periods, can affect all areas of your life. If you haven't yet looked at the first two chapters, now is the time to start at the beginning of the book and work your way through, implementing as many of the suggestions as appropriate for your life and circumstances. In particular, look at the meditation and relaxation elements in chapter 2 (see page 28).

Sitting down, feeling sorry for yourself and eating junk food – clearly the most tempting option – is only going to make you feel worse, so try to take some positive steps to dispel the stress.

Here are a few more suggestions to help you overcome the problem:

Caffeine: Cut down your caffeine intake. It can unsettle the nervous system.

Companionship: It is much easier to banish stress if you are in the company of a friend you can talk to and laugh with.

Exercise: Some people find that their usual exercise will help them deal with stress, whether that is something like yoga, which is specifically designed to aid relaxation, or something purely physical like a brisk walk or a game of squash.

Rest: Although it is good to exercise, don't overdo it. Stress can take it out of you physically, so do allow yourself rest and sleep.

Smile: It is quite bizarre, but it has been proved that not only is smiling infectious but that it actually helps you feel better, even if you have to force it. Try it and see for yourself.

Sunshine: Get out into the fresh air and sunlight, which can have a very uplifting effect. A brisk walk should be invigorating. By all means take some music or a podcast so that you have a distraction from your problems and allow yourself that time just to enjoy your surroundings.

Water: Drink plenty of water to flush toxins out of your system.

Wholefoods: Eat plenty of wholefoods, fish that are rich in omega-3 such as salmon, mackerel, herring, trout, sardines and tuna, and make sure you are including enough protein in your diet.

Try to identify the source of the stress because if you don't deal with the problem that is causing it, then it is bound to recur. Take positive action to deal with the problem if you can, or talk it through with a friend or a professional, such as your doctor.

Suncare
A gently golden tan looks and makes you feel good. But too much sun damages and ages the skin, even if you don't actually burn – which is to be avoided at all costs because it is painful and also does long-term damage.

Always use a high-protection-factor sunscreen, wear a sunhat and sunglasses, don't stay in the sun too long, and cover up much of the time. Take especial care with children's delicate skin. Be aware that you can still tan, and therefore burn, if you are in water, and that being in water will affect your sun cream, so reapply it regularly. Moisturize generously when you come out of the sun.

If you do get sunburn, try some aloe vera juice in a lukewarm bath, or dab the skin with some fresh cucumber slices.

Sweaty palms
If you are embarrassed by sweaty palms, rub some antiperspirant into your palms at night, before bed. Apply to completely dry skin.

KNOW WHAT TO DO IN AN EMERGENCY

Hopefully you will never need to use most of this information but, like any good insurance, if you take the precaution of knowing what to do in an emergency, it will pay out if you ever do need it.

This short section includes only the most basic information. It is not intended as a substitute for first-aid training, or even spending time on the websites of bodies such as the Red Cross and St John's Ambulance. These institutions also publish useful books and leaflets, both in print and download formats, as well as phone apps.

First-aid kit

A first-aid kit for the home only needs to include a few basic items to deal with minor injuries. It should be kept clean and accessible where you can easily lay hands on it. You should include:

first-aid guide;

antiseptic wipes and cleaning wipes;

assorted adhesive plasters;

disposable triangular bandage;

finger dressing;

small, medium and large non-stick dressings;

crêpe rolled bandage;

micropore tape;

disposable medical gloves;

foil blanket;

eyepad bandage;

eye wash and eye bath;

safety pins;

tweezers;

thermometer

instant ice pack;

scissors.

Basic first aid

Most small injuries can be dealt with using your first-aid kit and a little common sense. But what if something serious has happened? The first rule is that you should not put yourself at risk. It is no advantage to an injured person if you are also injured in your attempts to help them.

Check DR ABC (see below), an acronym that helps remind you how to take appropriate action. In a serious situation, call the emergency services immediately, otherwise do so when you have completed the check.

Danger: To the patient or yourself from, for example, traffic, fire, electricity. Check before proceeding.

Response: Is the patient conscious? Talk to the patient and see if they respond.

Airway: Is their airway blocked? Check there is nothing in their mouth.

Breathing: Are they breathing? Watch for movement and feel for air.

Circulation: Do they have a pulse? The best place to find a pulse is in the neck just to the left of centre.

The paramedics will need to know your name, exact location (postcode or zip code, if possible), contact telephone number, the number and condition of the injured and any specific hazards.

Bleeding

Call an ambulance. Elevate the wound and apply pressure.

Broken bones and dislocations

If a bone is broken, the patient may have a twisted limb, find movement difficult, feel a grating or swelling and be in severe pain. However, this is not always the case, so if in doubt, get it checked out.

Use common sense when it comes to getting expert help. If the patient is pretty mobile, perhaps with a broken finger, you could drive them to the local hospital, but if you suspect that the back, neck, a leg or hip is broken, for example, then you should call an ambulance. Support the injured part to keep it still. Keep the patient warm and reassured until expert help arrives.

Heart attack
This is caused by a blockage of the blood supply to the heart. The patient will suffer acute chest pain and possibly pain in the arm, pale skin, sweating and a weak, rapid pulse.

Call an ambulance. Sit the patient down as comfortably as possible, ideally on the floor leaning against a wall with knees bent and head and shoulders supported. Unless they are allergic to it, give the patient a 300mg aspirin to chew on slowly – it helps prevent clots and can be life-saving.

Shock
Any serious incident or injury can induce shock, which is a restriction of blood to the brain (this is a medical condition, it does not mean the person is simply 'shocked' by something). It manifests in a pale face, clammy skin, weak pulse, shallow breathing, confusion and sometimes loss of response. Call an ambulance. Lie the person down, keep them warm, loosen tight clothing and monitor and reassure them until expert help arrives.

Stroke
To check, act FAST:

Face: The patient can only smile on one side of their face.

Arms: They can only raise one arm.

Speech: Their speech is unclear.

Time: Time is of the essence. If you spot any of the above, call an ambulance. Keep the person warm and reassured until expert help arrives.

Unconscious

Call an ambulance. If the person is not breathing, administer CPR if you are trained to do so. Put the person in the recovery position.

Recovery position

While you wait for the ambulance, it is best if an unconscious patient is in the recovery position rather than on their back. However, do not move the patient if you suspect broken bones or neck or back injuries.

- Kneel next to them and place their nearest arm at right angles to their body, palm up.

- Place their other arm across their chest and hold the palm against the cheek nearest you.

- With your other hand, lift their far knee and put their foot flat on the floor. Gently pull the knee towards you to roll them on their side.

- Check that their airway is open.

The sooner the paramedics can reach the patient, the better the outcome is likely to be so call the emergency services as soon as possible, giving them as much accurate information as you can and delegate someone, if possible, to make sure your road is clear to reach the patient.

You are what you eat

How to get into the healthy eating habit

Food is fuel. If you are lucky enough to drive a Porsche – pause for laughter – you wouldn't fill it with paraffin. You need to use the best fuel you can so you get the best results. Your body is no different. Follow a healthy, balanced diet and you will feel healthier, look better and generally give yourself the best possible chance of staying fit, avoiding illness, maintaining a healthy weight and banishing stress.

SO WHAT IS A HEALTHY, BALANCED DIET?

Diet fads come and go, but the principles of a healthy diet are straightforward. Specific recommendations vary in different countries, but a good outline has been published by the British Food Standards Agency. Their eat-well plate is a visual representation of a healthy balanced diet that makes it easy to see what you should be eating and in what proportions. It won't apply to every meal individually, but over the course of a few days, or a week, this is the balance to aim for.

Eat well plate

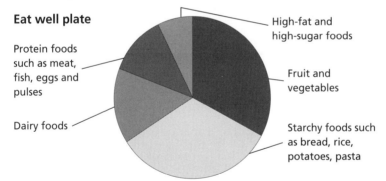

Protein foods such as meat, fish, eggs and pulses

Dairy foods

High-fat and high-sugar foods

Fruit and vegetables

Starchy foods such as bread, rice, potatoes, pasta

To make sure fresh foods are at the optimum nutritional value, try to eat locally produced ingredients in season where possible. If you buy foods that are out of season, they will have been brought in from abroad or forced locally and will have lost a lot of their goodness in the process, no matter how well they are treated. The greater the food miles, the greater the environmental impact, too, as they will have incurred transport-cost and energy implications. (Obviously, there are exceptions – you don't see many banana plantations in Scotland, for example!)

Fruit and vegetables
Medical evidence suggests that we eat **at least** five helpings of fruit and vegetables a day, probably more, to make up one-third of our food intake. They can be fresh, frozen, canned, dried or juiced (to a maximum of 150ml/5 fl oz/²/₃ cup a day). With the range now available in markets and supermarkets, that's not too difficult.

They supply nutrients, vitamins and minerals to keep the body in good health, and fibre to maintain a healthy digestive system.

Slow-release carbohydrates
Rice, bread, potatoes, pasta and other starchy foods should also make up about one-third of our food. Wholegrain and brown varieties retain all their nutrients so are the best choice. White rice, for example, has been stripped of the outer layer of the grain that contains much of the nutrient value.

Starchy foods make an essential contribution to the diet by providing the main source of energy as well as other crucial nutrients.

Dairy foods
Milk, yogurt and other dairy foods, or alternatives such as soy milk and yogurts, should make up about one-sixth of our diet.

They provide fats, protein and other nutrients, such as calcium.

Protein
Meat, fish, nuts and pulses are all good sources of protein, which should make up about one-eighth of our food intake.

Protein is essential for cell growth and provides essential vitamins and minerals.

Fat-rich and sugar-rich foods
Contrary to popular myth, we need fat in our diet, not just for flavour, but

to protect our organs and maintain body temperature. Fat is an important energy source that also gives us essential vitamins. However, it is better to meet your fat requirements from unsaturated or monounsaturated fats, and in the correct proportion.

Sugar is not essential, but is not harmful in small quantities.

What are the benefits of a healthy diet?

Making sure your body is given the benefits of the best possible nourishment is bound to allow it to perform at its best and you should look forward to the following benefits:

- Shiny, strong hair.

- Strong nails.

- Clear skin.

- Fewer colds and minor illnesses.

- Potentially less likelihood of developing type 2 diabetes and other serious conditions.

- More energy.

- Good sleep patterns.

- Healthy weight.

EXPLODING THE MYTHS

First, let's dispense with a few of the myths surrounding healthy eating and, since obesity is such a major issue, slimming diets. The nature of media reporting is that it often focuses on one aspect – something new and exciting – rather than looking at the bigger picture. After all, the eat-well plate has been around for a long time and is not 'news' any more, while the latest fad diet that has been a brilliant success for some minor celebrity will make a story.

Is it only about calories?

A calorie is simply a unit of energy. If you regularly eat more calories than you burn in energy, then you will put on weight. The number of calories you need is based on your height, gender, age and level of activity. However, to be healthy, you need those calories to be coming from all the major food groups in the right proportions, as we've seen. A slice of chocolate fudge cake has a disproportionately large number of calories for the nutritional benefit it offers.

Is butter bad?

Butter is not bad. In fact, it is far better than many spreads because it is a naturally made product with no artificial ingredients – unlike many other spreads that need a large label so there's room to list everything that goes into them. The point with fats is that they should be eaten in the right quantities and proportions and ideally most of your fat intake should be of unsaturated fats, so butter is something to be enjoyed in moderation.

Are carbs bad?

Carbohydrates are not bad, although slow-release carbohydrates – from oats, bananas, wholemeal bread, brown rice, and so on – are the best choice. Carbohydrates should make up no more than 33 per cent (one third) of our food intake. We need them to fuel our bodies.

Will sugar kill you?

There is an element of truth to the belief that sugar can kill. We do not need refined sugar in our diet at all – it is called 'empty calories', which means it provides no nutritional value. It is better to avoid refined sugar, and if you eat fresh foods cooked from scratch, that is the easiest way to do so, because then there is no danger of consuming the high quantities of sugar 'hidden' in processed foods. Look at the labels when you are buying not only dessert foods but ready-meals and any other processed foods. You will be surprised how much sugar you'll find. If you are cooking for yourself, you won't add sugar to savoury foods and you can sweeten desserts with honey or fruit instead.

Is fat the enemy?

Fat is not the enemy; it is an essential part of the diet. However, it should be eaten in the right proportions, as we have seen, and come mainly from unsaturated sources.

Can fad diets help you lose weight?

Common sense simply isn't 'news', therefore the media latch onto one new craze after another and skew the picture. Fad diets can have a short-term impact, but as they do not teach you to eat a healthy balanced diet, they will not succeed in the long run because you will simply return to your old eating habits.

FIND YOUR INCENTIVE

We have already seen that it is not easy to break established habits and, for most of us, that's what we need to do if we are going to improve our diet and therefore our health. Since that is never easy, try to come up with your own incentive to keep you on the path towards where you want your body shape to be. That objective shouldn't be totally unrealistic. Aim high but not so high that you can never succeed. If you have an objective, it can help to keep you going when your will power starts to flag. It might be an event – a wedding, perhaps – when you want to look your best. You might be determined to get back to the clothing size you wore a few years ago. You might be joining a new club and want to look and feel your best. You might simply be aware that your weight is creeping up and you need to take back control.

So what if you can't find an incentive? You enjoy food, you don't vastly over-eat, the balance of your diet isn't bad. That's probably the hardest scenario. You might benefit from joining a slimming group, or teaming up with a friend so you can encourage each other. Another motivator is to list all the positive benefits of losing excess weight and getting healthier. See how long the list is in comparison with the downsides and that should keep you going.

Most people know when they feel in the correct weight range but this table shows the various height/weight ratios.

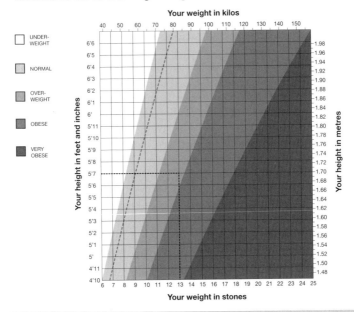

Your weight in kilos

UNDER-WEIGHT

NORMAL

OVER-WEIGHT

OBESE

VERY OBESE

Your height in feet and inches

Your height in metres

Your weight in stones

START WITH SOME SIMPLE CHANGES

To start with, make a few simple observations of how you eat, which should highlight the areas you need to change and why. Don't be in too much of a rush; slow and steady is far more likely to win the race. Begin with small adjustments to set you on the right path without overturning everything you are used to. And remember that you are aiming to try to adjust your eating habits, not just follow a regime for a few weeks or months.

Some people eat large portions; some graze all day. Carbs are popular with some, protein with others. Skipping breakfast is common. Eating late is also much quoted. Jot down your eating pattern and think about which elements are not doing you any favours.

- Aim to eat three meals a day and avoid snacking.

- If you tend to eat portions that you know are too large, use a smaller plate.

- If you are not sure of your proportions, use a permanent marker to mark the segments of the eat-well plate on a plate to help you serve your food in the correct balance. Not every meal will include all the elements but it's a useful guide.

- If you are in the habit of snacking, replace biscuits with nuts, seeds or fruit – such as an apple or a banana.

- Try to drink at least 1.5 litres (2½ pints/6 cups) of water every day. Some people recommend even more to flush out toxins and keep your body hydrated.

- Cut out, if possible, or cut down refined sugar.

- Try to cut down on the amount of fatty food you consume.

- Increase your protein intake and include some oily fish – such as salmon, mackerel and herring – at least once a week.

- Grill (broil) food on a rack instead of frying it.

- Eat more casseroles and steamed foods.

- Reduce your caffeine intake.

- Reduce your alcohol intake.

- Exercise daily for half an hour.

Water

We all know we should probably drink more water, but how many of us actually swig the quantity of water doctors and beauty writers tell us is essential for our health and appearance? Why not establish a regime of sipping a glass of water on the hour every hour, from eight in the morning until three in the afternoon? It won't be long until you feel the benefit.

In many places tap water is perfectly safe and tastes good. If you are in an area where this is not the case, then you will need to drink bottled water.

Moving on

As you get used to your new routine, you can start to introduce more variety, perhaps cut down on your intake of red meats and begin to introduce some more unusual ingredients, including many of the so-called superfoods (see below).

SUPERFOODS A TO Z

Superfoods is a term coined by the media with no strict scientific definition. What these foods share in common is that they have high levels of beneficial antioxidants, polyphenols, vitamins and minerals.

There is some scientific evidence, and much anecdotal evidence, for their efficacy, especially for those ingredients that have been used in the Far East and South America for thousands of years. Claims that they can prevent or cure serious illness, such as cancer, are not proven but incorporating them into your diet can only be good.

Acai: A small purple berry that is high in antioxidants and great for smoothies.

Apples: High in cancer-reducing antioxidants.

Asparagus: Contains vitamin K for strong bones and folate (folic acid/vitamin B9) to combat bloating.

Avocados: Contain healthy fats that help the body process other nutrients.

Bananas: For fibre and slow-release carbohydrates.

Barley: Excellent source of fibre.

Black beans: Full of antioxidants for healthy arteries, plus fibre and protein.

Black garlic: Made from fermented garlic bulbs, it brings properties that stabilize gut flora and also provides essential probiotics.

Blackberries: Rich in antioxidants.

Blueberries: High in antioxidants and vitamin C. Antioxidants are good for the memory and communication between brain cells.

Bok choy: Calcium-rich for bone protection.

Brazil nuts: Optimum source of selenium, which helps the immune system and fertility.

Broccoli: Rich source of vitamin C and folic acid and may contain a cancer-suppressing phytonutrient.

Brown rice: Full of fibre and magnesium to support efficient chemical reactions in the body.

Brussels sprouts: Contain compounds that detoxify the body.

Cacao: Antioxidants in raw cacao help lower blood pressure.

Cauliflower: High in anti-cancer compounds.

Celery: Contains essential oils that fight ageing and regulate the nervous system, as well as anti-cancer and detox compounds.

Chia seeds: Packed with omega-3 fatty acids, fibre and calcium plus other nutrients.

Edamame: These are young soybeans, which are high in protein and fibre and help lower cholesterol.

Eggs: Low in calories but high in protein, versatile and the ideal breakfast.

Flaxseed: Packed with omega-3 fatty acids and anti-cancer compounds.

Goji berries: High in vitamin C and antioxidants, these berries support the immune system and improve circulation.

Grapes: Both red and white grapes make refreshing, low-calorie snacks but red or purple grapes contain more flavonoids (antioxidants) than white ones (the darker the better) which can help protect against osteoporosis, some cancers and cardiovascular diseases.

Greek yogurt: High in protein and low in fat. Buy Greek yogurt, not Greek-style yogurt.

Green tea: For healthy arteries.

Hemp seeds: High in protein and amino acids, and supplying omega-6 and omega-3 fatty acids.

Kale: Full of vitamin K and anti-cancer nutrients.

Kefir: This slightly sour probiotic yogurt drink improves digestive health and supports the immune system.

Kiwi fruit: High in vitamin C.

Lentils: Packed with protein.

Maca powder: Reduces fatigue.

Mangosteen: The white middle of this tropical fruit contains potassium and a powerful antioxidant and can help combat inflammation.

Milk: Contains calcium for strong bones, vitamin D and muscle-building protein.

Nutritional yeast: Made from deactivated yeast, this food supplement is a source of vitamin B12, protein and fibre.

Oats: Excellent slow-release carbohydrates that also contain fibre, phytonutrients and minerals to help lower cholesterol and prevent heart disease.

Olives: Low in calories but contain monounsaturated fat for heart health.

Oranges: For vitamin C, calcium and folate (folic acid/vitamin B9).

Oysters: Eat these for iron, zinc and selenium.

Peanut butter: For healthy blood vessels. Ideally buy the pure ones with no added salt or sugar.

Potatoes, baked: Rich in potassium to lower blood pressure.

Prunes: Good for the digestion and contain polyphenols that stimulate bone-building cells.

Pumpkin: High in alpha- and beta-carotene, natural cancer fighters.

Rapeseed (canola) oil: Good for the heart and contains vitamin E.

Salmon: Contains omega-3 fatty acids, B vitamins and selenium, good for circulation, cutting cancer risk and reducing cholesterol.

Scallops: High in protein and low in calories.

Seaweed: Packed with omega-3 fatty acids and minerals, which guard against heart attack and stroke.

Shiitake mushrooms: For vitamin D.

Soya milk: Contains calcium, vitamin D and protein.

Spinach: Full of vitamin K, good for strong bones and efficient blood clotting.

Spring greens and collard greens: Plenty of vitamin A and other compounds essential for eye health.

Strawberries: Heavy in anti-cancer phytochemicals.

Sunflower seeds: For heart-healthy vitamin E.

Sweet potatoes: Rich in vitamin A to support your immune system and healthy vision.

Tomatoes: High in vitamin C, antioxidants and fibre, and can lower cholesterol and protect against UV rays and lower cholesterol.

Turkey breast: High in protein for very few calories.

Walnuts: Packed with omega-3 fatty acids that support memory and concentration.

Watercress: Low in calories but high in vitamin K and anti-cancer substances.

A WORD ABOUT PLANNING

If your food cupboard is full of white flour, sugar, sugar-rich preserves and so on, then you will reach for them when you get hungry and all your good intentions will go out of the window.

Sort out your pantry and get rid of all the things you are going to substitute. (Rather than waste them, you may want to do a batch bake and freeze some treats that you can enjoy as an occasional indulgence.) Gradually rebuild your stock cupboard with a selection of healthy nuts, seeds, cans and dried goods. That way you will always be able to rustle up a meal or a snack that's good for you.

Plan your meals through the week so that, between them, the proportions roughly follow the eat-well plate (see page 77). Make a list of what you need and head over to your favourite store, preferably when you are not hungry, as that would encourage you to pick up a few little tasty things that will not do you much good.

Watch out for special offers but make sure you only go for those that really benefit you. If they help you save money, special offers are great. But if they encourage you to buy things that will be wasted, or to buy more cakes, fizzy drinks and biscuits than you can resist – not so good.

STORING FOOD

Correct storage will retain the nutrients in your food and keep it fresh for longer so you enjoy it more, it is better for you and you waste less.

A date on everything

Sell-by, use-by, best-before dates – what do they all mean? And how much attention should you pay to them? Fortunately, there is a simple answer: pay attention to exactly what they are saying – they actually *say what they mean* and they don't all mean the same thing – but be guided by your common sense.

Remember that canned and bottled goods are rarely a problem.

- **Sell-by** is the date the shop wants the product off its shelves – but it will still be perfect for at least a week.

- In every case, the manufacturers and stores err on the side of caution, so if you buy something on its sell-by date, for example, it should still be fine in a few days' time.

- **Best-before** means only that the product is likely to start to deteriorate from perfect quality at that point.

- **Use-by** date is the date you should have finished eating the product.

- All products are different. Be cautious with fish and especially seafood, pâté, pork and chicken.

Storage tips

Bacon: Roll up slices instead of leaving them flat and they'll be less likely to stick together.

Bananas: Store separately as they will over-ripen other fruit. However, if you have some avocados that you are trying to ripen, put bananas with them to speed up the process. See page 98 for ideas on using up ripe bananas.

Bread: Try a celery stalk in the bread bin to keep your bread fresher longer.

Carrots: Cut off the green tops as soon as possible because they draw moisture away from the root.

Cheese: Keep in foil, not plastic wrapping, to avoid it sweating.

Cookies: A couple of sugar lumps in a cookie jar will absorb moisture and keep the cookies fresh.

Lemons or oranges: Store in a plastic box in the refrigerator. Leave to come back to room temperature before squeezing or eating. You can even slightly warm a lemon in the microwave to encourage it to yield more juice.

Lettuce: Use wooden or plastic salad cutters and servers as metal will turn the edges of the lettuce brown.

Onions: Store separately, especially away from eggs, which are porous and will absorb the onion flavour.

Passata (sieved tomatoes): Freeze leftovers in ice-cube trays then use from frozen as needed.

Peaches: Will ripen in a box covered in newspaper.

Pears: Will ripen in a paper bag with a ripe apple.

Pepper: Keep a few peppercorns in your ground pepper pot to prevent the holes from clogging up.

Salad leaves: Store in an unsealed plastic bag in the refrigerator.

Salt: A few grains of raw rice in a salt cellar will absorb moisture and stop the salt clogging up.

Sauces: To prevent a skin forming, cover with a layer of cling film (plastic wrap), making sure this touches the surface, before you put them in the refrigerator.

Strawberries: Keep in a fine-mesh strainer in a bowl in the refrigerator to allow the air to circulate around them.

Vanilla pod (bean): Once you have used the seeds, put the pod in a screw-topped jar of sugar to give it flavour. Similarly, store sugar with citrus rinds, to flavour it for use in baking.

Use the freezer
It makes it a great deal easier to stack things in the freezer if you freeze them in small rectangular plastic boxes. Make sure you label and date them – you'd be surprised how similar things look when they are frozen solid. Freeze in portions relevant to the size of your family and your lifestyle. For example, if one of you tends to eat at different times, then freeze at least some in individual portions.

BASIC COOKING METHODS

There are various ways of applying heat to cook food. If you know the basic principles, you can adapt them to cook anything in the most efficient way.

Boiling

Suitable for all kinds of food but used mostly for vegetables, rice and pasta. Put hard (root) vegetables in cold water and bring to the boil; add soft vegetables (greens) to already-boiling water. Reduce to a simmer and cook hard vegetables until just tender when you insert a knife but still crisp.

Steaming

Set up a steamer (on the hob or use an electric steamer) or put the food in a colander over a pan of boiling water. Cover and cook in the rising steam until tender. This is a gentle cooking method suitable for all kinds of food including vegetables, fish, dumplings and meat. It tends to retain the colour and flavour of vegetables better than boiling.

Grilling (broiling)

An option for quick-cooking cuts of meat that gives a lovely browned finish. Put the food under a grill (broiler) or on a barbecue, turning the food at least once, until tender and browned on the outside.

Frying

Another quick and convenient cooking method for meat, fish, eggs and vegetables, but try to avoid frying too often. Heat a little oil in a frying pan on the hob – use sunflower, groundnut (peanut) or rapeseed (canola) oil as they maintain temperature better than olive oil – and cook over a medium-high heat until the food is browned on the outside and cooked through, turning as necessary.

For deep-frying, fill a heavy-based pan one-third full of oil and heat over a high heat until the oil bubbles around the handle of a wooden spoon. Gently lower the food into the pan and fry, turning, until crisp. Never leave the pan unattended. Lift out the cooked food with a slotted spoon or wire basket and drain on paper towels before serving.

Stir-fry over a very high heat, tossing and stirring the food so that it cooks quickly and evenly.

Baking

Used mainly for cakes and breads, this is cooking dry in an oven, usually at about 180°C (350°F/gas mark 4).

Roasting

Another method of cooking meat, fish or vegetables in the oven, this time in fat either at a high temperature (200°C/400°F/gas mark 6) for a crisp finish, or slowly (at 160°C/325°F/gas mark 3) for longer-cooked, tender results.

Braising, stewing or casseroling

Similar to boiling, all these mean cooking in a liquid sauce. Braising is done in a shallow sauce in the oven, stewing in plenty of sauce on the hob, and casseroling in plenty of sauce in the oven. These are slow methods of cooking meat, fish and vegetables and therefore give very tender results. The oven temperature should be low, about 160°C/325°F/gas mark 3, or the pan kept over a low heat, with a lid on the pan. You can also use an electric slow cooker.

BASIC RECIPES

If you understand the basic principles of cooking, you can go to recipes for ideas and inspiration but don't need to follow them slavishly. That way, if a recipe calls for courgette (zucchini) and you have pumpkin, you'll know you can substitute one for the other and get a similar result. One important thing to do is to taste the food as you go. You'll soon get used to adding some more salt and pepper or a dash of sauce and will be able to adjust the recipe to suit your taste.

Here are some very basic recipes for you to use as a starting point for your own ideas.

Soups

Chop an onion, a celery stalk, a carrot and a garlic clove and fry gently in a little oil in a saucepan for about ten minutes until soft. Add some stock and your main ingredient, a little salt and pepper and perhaps some herbs and spices and simmer until the ingredients are tender. Blitz in a blender, if you like.

Some suggestions: carrot and coriander; tomato and basil; parsnip and lemon; mushroom and prawn; lentil and coconut milk; mixed vegetable.

Salads

Crisp, fresh and colourful – that's what an enticing salad should be. Lettuce doesn't even have to feature, although mixed salad leaves make a great salad base. Don't include too many items – three or four is plenty.

You can also add seafood, cold meats and cheeses to turn a salad from a side dish into a main lunch dish. Add crusty bread to make it more substantial.

A dressing will really enhance a salad. Go easy on the mayonnaise as it is high in fats; try a vinaigrette dressing or a drizzle of balsamic vinegar.

Some suggestions: tomato, basil and mozzarella; grated carrot and beetroot (beet); celery, chorizo and walnut; mixed leaves with cucumber.

Eggs

So versatile and nutritious, there are plenty of things you can do with eggs.

Boiled eggs: Put the eggs in a pan and cover with cold water. Add a pinch of salt and a splash of vinegar (these will set the egg if the shell cracks). Bring to the boil, then boil for 3 minutes, remove from the pan with a slotted spoon and serve. For hard-boiled eggs, boil for 8 minutes, then lift out and plunge into cold water to cool quickly – this prevents the edge of the yolk going grey. (Timings may vary, depending on the size and freshness of your eggs.)

Fried eggs: Heat a little oil in a frying pan, break in the egg, cover and fry for a few minutes until crisp on the base and the white is just set. You can splash the oil over the top of the egg to speed up cooking if you like.

Omelette: Heat a little oil in a frying pan while you whisk 2 or 3 eggs with some salt and pepper and a dash of milk. Pour into the pan. As the bottom starts to set, lift up the sides so the uncooked mixture on top runs underneath. Either flip the omelette over to cook the other side, or add some chopped ham, mushrooms or other ingredients and fold the omelette in half.

Poached eggs: Bring a pan of water to the boil. Break a fresh egg into a cup, then gently slide the egg into the boiling water. Cook for about 3 minutes until the white is set, then lift out with a slotted spoon.

Pancakes: Whisk 100g (4oz/1 cup) plain (all-purpose) flour, 300ml (10fl oz/1¼ cups) milk, 2 eggs and a pinch of salt, then leave to stand for 30 minutes or more. Whisk again. Heat a little oil in a frying pan, then pour in enough of the batter to cover the pan, tilting the pan as you pour so it spreads thinly over the base. Fry for a couple of minutes, then flip over and cook the other side. Keep the pancakes warm while you cook the remaining batter, adding more oil as necessary. Serve with honey and lemon, or fill with sweet or savoury options and roll up.

Scrambled eggs: Whisk 2 eggs in a bowl with as pinch of salt while you heat a knob of butter in a pan. Add the eggs and keep stirring over a low heat for about 3 minutes until scrambled but still moist.

Stews and casseroles
Start a stew or casserole in the same way as a soup, frying your onion and vegetables until soft. Add your chosen meat or vegetables and fry until browned. Add a splash of wine, if you like, and cook until it evaporates. Stir in some tomato purée (paste) and some herbs, then add just enough stock to cover the main ingredients. Bring to the boil, cover and simmer or cook in a low oven for at least an hour until tender and thickened.

Some suggestions: chicken with thyme and vegetables; beef, tomato and mushroom; pork, beans and parsley; sausage, bacon and tomato.

Rice and pasta
Measure one mug of rice for every four people and add twice as much water. Bring to the boil, then simmer gently for about 8 minutes until the water has almost all been absorbed. Put on the lid tightly, or cover with foil and put on the lid. Remove from the heat and leave to stand somewhere warm for 15 minutes. Fork through and serve.

Add 2 handfuls of pasta per person to a pan of boiling water. Return to the boil and simmer until 'al dente' – just tender but not soggy. Fresh pasta will only take a couple of minutes; dried pasta will take 8–10 minutes. Serve as it is, or stir through some pesto sauce; egg and cream; cooked ham and vegetables.

Cake

A basic cake is made up of equal quantities of butter, sugar and flour with some eggs – then varied infinitely! All you need do is heat the oven to 180°C (350°F/gas mark 4) and grease and line a 20cm (8in) cake tin (pan). Put 100g (4oz/½ cup) self-raising flour in a bowl with 100g (4oz/½ cup) soft butter, 100g (4oz/1 cup) sugar and 2 eggs and mix (with an electric mixer, if you have one) until light and pale. The mixture should be quite soft, and drop off the spoon with a nice 'splodge' when you knock a spoon on the side of the bowl (that's called the dropping consistency). Spoon into the prepared pan and bake for 30 minutes until springy in the middle and the cake is pulling away from the side of the pan.

If you like, you can change the butter for oil, add some cocoa powder or other flavours, and/or mix in some chocolate chips or fruit chunks. You can also use the mix to make fairy cakes simply by dividing it between small cake cases (reduce the cooking time) then sprinkle with nuts and drizzle with a little honey.

For a basic butter icing, blend some butter with twice its weight in icing (confectioners') sugar – 75g (3oz/⅓ cup) butter is plenty for the top of a 20cm (8in) cake – and mix thoroughly until blended.

Pimp it up

It is easy to improve on ready-made products by adding a little extra flavouring or other ingredients. For example, liven up soups or stews with a dash of Worcestershire sauce, pomegranate molasses, tomato ketchup or tomato purée (paste); sprinkle with some herbs, salt and pepper; add a splash of sherry or red wine.

Soften the flavour of a dish with a spoonful of yogurt or crème fraîche, especially a hot curry. You can also use sour cream (or cream with a teaspoon of lemon juice added) for every 300ml (10fl oz/1¼ cups).

Eke it out
More people than you expected to lunch?

- Add some breadcrumbs to a minced-meat dish.

- Rinse and drain a can or two of pulses and add to a dish.

- Sprinkle the top with some grated cheese or grated carrot.

- Cook plenty of extra vegetables.

- Serve with some crusty bread.

USING UP LEFTOVERS

In tune with our intention not to waste energy, food waste is a huge problem in the developed countries and we should all be doing our bit to reduce the amount of food simply thrown away, both in our homes and by the supermarkets (see pages 35–6).

If you have a lot of leftovers, perhaps you are cooking too much in the first place. Try reducing your portion sizes gradually until you have less left on the plates. Of course, if you have extra portions, you can freeze them to provide a quick meal in the future.

If you aim to use leftover ingredients by making them into tasty and nutritious dishes, you be wasting less and saving more money, too. Here are a few ideas for foods that are commonly left over. But remember, whether you reheat in the oven, the microwave, on a heatproof plate above a pan of simmering water or in a saucepan, always make sure food heats for at least ten minutes and is piping hot throughout. Do not reheat more than once, especially fish, poultry and meat.

Bananas
There is no need to throw out bananas that are slightly brown. They have a delicious natural sweetness.

Banana bread: Mix 250g (9oz/2½ cups) of plain flour, 1 teaspoon bicarbonate of soda (baking soda) and 1 teaspoon of baking powder in a bowl. Add 4 tablespoons of honey, 3 large eggs, 150ml (5fl oz/²/₃ cup) of yogurt and 3 mashed bananas and mix together gently. Turn into a greased and lined 900g (2lb) loaf pan and sprinkle with 2 tablespoons of chopped walnuts. Bake in a preheated oven at 160°C (325°F/gas mark 3) for an hour until a skewer inserted in the middle comes out clean.

Banana milkshakes and smoothies: Blend a banana with milk, a teaspoon of honey, if you like, and perhaps a pinch of cinnamon. For variety, add different fruits – such as blueberries or raspberries – stir in some ice cream, and make as thick as you like.

Banana muffins: Mix 225g (8oz/1½ cups) of plain flour and 2 teaspoons of baking powder in a bowl and make a well in the middle. Mix 2 tablespoons of honey, 225ml (8fl oz/1 cup) milk and 120ml (4fl oz/½ cup) sunflower oil and stir in until almost combined. Gently stir in a mashed banana. Spoon into muffin cases and bake at 200°C (400°F/gas mark 6) for about 20 minutes until springy to the touch.

Banana pancakes: Blend 100g (4oz/1 cup) of plain flour with 2 eggs, 300ml (10½fl oz/1¼ cups) of milk and a banana to a thick batter, adding a little more milk if the mixture is too thick. Fry a ladleful at a time in a hot, lightly greased pan.

Bread
There are so many things to do with bread that is just beginning to go stale (not mouldy!) that it never needs to be wasted.

Bread and butter pudding: Butter the slices and layer them in an ovenproof dish, sprinkling each layer with a little sugar and some sultanas. Whisk an egg into a jug of milk and pour it over the bread until it comes three-quarters of the way up the dish. Leave to stand for at least 30 minutes, then bake at 180°C (350°F/gas mark 4) for about an hour until crisp on top and soft underneath.

Breadcrumbs: Blitz the bread in a blender or food processor to make breadcrumbs and store them in the freezer. Use them for coating chicken or other meats and vegetables, thickening casseroles, or mixing with melted butter to use as flan bases.

Croûtons: Cut bread into small cubes and fry or toast until crisp. Serve with soups or sprinkled on salads.

French toast: Dip the bread slices in beaten egg and fry on both sides until golden.

Mini bread-based pizzas: Cut sliced bread into circles and toast on one side. Blitz some cherry tomatoes, tomato purée (paste), a few herbs and a little salt and pepper to a paste in a food processor, spread on the untoasted side of the bread and top with grated cheese, then brown under the grill (broiler).

Stuffing: Make breadcrumbs (see above) and mix with a chopped onion, chopped sage and an egg then season with salt and pepper. Roll into balls and fry or bake.

Fish
Try these ideas or add to a stir-fry (see page 92).

Couscous: Make a bowl of couscous and stir through some cooked fish, vegetables and a dash of seasoning or chopped fresh herbs.

Fish cakes: Mix equal quantities of mashed potato and cooked fish and roll into patties. Coat in beaten egg, then breadcrumbs and fry until piping hot and crisp on both sides.

Fish pie: Make a white sauce with 1 tablespoon of butter, 1 tablespoon of cornflour (corn starch) and 300ml (10½fl oz/1¼ cups) of milk, stirring until thick. Stir in 1 tablespoon of tomato purée (paste) and some salt and pepper. Stir in the chunks of fish, then pour into an ovenproof dish. Top with mashed potatoes and bake in the oven at 200°C (400°F/gas mark 6) for half an hour until piping hot and crisp on top.

Chicken
Cold chicken is delicious in salads and sandwiches and is quite safe to cook for a second time as long as you make sure it is thoroughly heated all the way through.

Chicken stir-fry: Stir-fry in a little hot oil with chopped onion and vegetables. Add a little soy sauce and mirin for an oriental flavour.

Spicy chicken burgers: Mince the meat and mix with chopped onion, breadcrumbs, chopped garlic, salt and pepper and an egg. Shape into patties and fry in hot oil until cooked through and browned.

Chicken and leek pie: Make a sauce with 1 tablespoon of butter, 1 tablespoon of plain/all-purpose flour, 300ml (10fl oz/1¼ cups) of milk, 1 tablespoon of tomato purée (paste) and a stock (bouillon) cube. Mix in the chopped chicken and pour into an ovenproof dish. Top with a sheet of puff or shortcrust pastry, brush with milk, then bake in a preheated oven at 200°C (400°F/gas mark 6) for about 30 minutes until golden.

Lamb or beef
Serve cold and sliced with pickles or chop into a couscous salad. Alternatively, make some gravy, warm the meat through in the gravy and serve with your favourite vegetables.

Shepherd's or cottage pie: Mince the meat and mix with some gravy. Top with mashed potato and bake until heated through and browned on top.

Curry: Dice the meat and add to a curry sauce to serve with rice.

Stir-fry: Dice the meat and add to stir-fries (see page 92).

Spicy kebabs: Chop into chunks to thread onto skewers. Brush with a mixture of 1 tablespoon of honey, 1 tablespoon of soy sauce and a dash of lemon juice then grill (broil) until hot and sticky.

Rice
Stir-fried rice: Heat a little oil in a wok or large pan and fry a chopped onion and garlic clove until soft. Add the rice, a few peas and any leftover vegetables and stir until heated through. Add a few drops of soy sauce, some chopped herbs or other ingredients or flavourings.

Vegetables
Try some of these ideas, add to couscous or salads, or make up your own recipes for using up leftover vegetables.

Bubble and squeak: Chop or mash and mix together leftover mashed, roast or boiled potatoes, Brussels sprouts, onions, parsnips. You can include bits of bacon, sausage, other meat – whatever you have available. Heat the mixture in the oven until hot. Heat a little oil in a large frying pan and finish off the bubble and squeak by frying in the pan until it has a lovely brown crust.

Casserole: Add leftover vegetables to a stew or casserole that you are cooking to bulk it out.

Quick stir-fry: Cut the veg into even-sized pieces and stir-fry in hot oil until browned.

Roasted vegetables: Make sure the vegetables are in evenly sized pieces and spread in an ovenproof dish, toss with oil and roast in a hot oven until heated through and browned.

Vegetable soup: Add to stock with a few herbs and some lentils and simmer until tender. Blitz with a food processor until smooth, if you like.

Help around the home

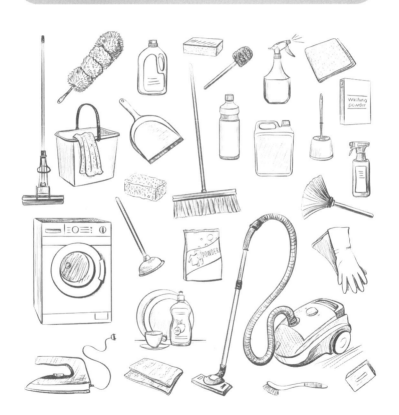

Simple ways to de-stress the household chores

Once you have decluttered your home and everything has its own place, the only thing left to do is make sure you put things back where they belong when you have used them. If you try to get into the habit of not leaving things lying around, you should soon find that it becomes second nature. The number of people who love cleaning the house is – I venture to suggest – fairly small. But it has to be done, and most of us like a reasonably clean and tidy house. What we don't need, if we are going to stay calm and enjoy life to the full, is – you guessed it – to stress over it.

Firstly, ask yourself how much it matters if the house is a bit untidy or the washing up hasn't been done? It is your home, after all, and living involves making a mess at times. Besides which, a house can be too tidy. It is so uncomfortable to be in a house where you don't dare sit down for fear of squashing the beautifully plumped cushions. There is a desirable happy medium between having a kitchen floor you could eat off and growing penicillin in the coffee cups.

MAKE IT EASY ON YOURSELF

The best way to do housework is the least stressful one for you. Most people start at the top, with the bedrooms. Some people complete a room at a time, others go through the whole house doing one thing at a time: feather duster for reaching up to the ceiling, dusters for easy-to-reach surfaces, hoovering, and so on. I'm a room-at-a-time person and my basic sequence is:

- Tidy up.
- Empty the bins.
- Dust and polish.
- Vacuum.

Special jobs can be spread out so you are not doing them all at once: change the sheets, turn and vacuum the mattress, clean the windows.

Try to make each job more pleasurable by putting some music or the radio on while you work – whistle or sing along! Make everyone in the household contribute – there's no reason why one person should have to do everything.

CLEANING HINTS AND TIPS

Cleaning products can be expensive and sometimes toxic, so use them carefully and add a little elbow grease to make things go further. You might find that some old-fashioned remedies work better than the new ones, although there are some products that do bring us the benefits of research and technology!

For the kitchen

All-purpose cleaner: Mix two tablespoons of bicarbonate of soda (baking soda) with 600ml (1 pint/2½ cups) of warm water, the juice of ½ lemon and 1 tablespoon white vinegar in a spray bottle.

Blenders: To clean out a blender, half-fill it with hot water and add a few drops of detergent. Put on the lid and switch it on for a minute. Then rinse it with warm water.

Brass: Polish brass with a paste of lemon juice and salt. Rinse clean and buff up to a shine. Alternatively, smear the brass with brown sauce and then buff with half a lemon dipped in salt. For brass taps, use a little mild washing-up liquid and rinse with cold water, or wash them with white spirit.

Bread bins: If your bread bin becomes mildewed, wipe it with a cloth soaked in vinegar and leave the bin empty with the lid open until the smell has gone completely.

Burned-on food: Don't try to scrape badly burned-on food off pots and pans. Soak them overnight in hot water and biological washing powder. The residue will float off when you wash them the next morning.

Dishwasher: Keep the inside of your dishwasher immaculate by filling the detergent container with citric acid (you should be able to buy this from your pharmacy) and running the machine with no dishes in it. If you can't get citric acid, use lemon juice.

Drains: If your drains are giving off a nasty odour, pour some bicarbonate of soda (baking soda) followed by a cupful of vinegar directly down the plughole. Put the plug in and leave the two components to react with one another for about 30 minutes. Pour a kettle full of boiling water down the drain to wash away any residue.

Kettles: If you find your kettle has become furred up with a build-up of limescale, half fill it with equal quantities of water and vinegar and boil. Once the water has boiled, leave it for about 15 minutes, then rinse it out thoroughly and boil with clean water a couple of times so it is really clean and any taste of vinegar has gone.

Non-stick pans: Boiling water with a little bleach and vinegar before rinsing and washing can normally clean grubby non-stick pans. After doing this, you'll need to grease them with a little olive oil to keep them non-stick.

Ovens: Keep your oven smelling sweet by baking old lemon and orange rinds in it occasionally at 180°C (350°F/gas mark 4) for 30 minutes. To clean your oven, mix five tablespoons of bicarbonate of soda (baking soda), a few drops of liquid soap and four tablespoons of white vinegar to a thick paste and apply it to the inside of the oven. Scrub any stubborn marks with an abrasive sponge and then rinse and wipe clean.

For especially greasy ovens, mix equal quantities of lemon juice and salt to a paste and spread over the area. Leave for 30 minutes, scrub with an abrasive sponge, rinse and wipe the oven clean.

If something has been spilt in a hot oven, cover the affected area with salt and when the oven is cool, the residue should simply lift off.

Plastic tables and worktops: For a spotlessly clean and shining surface, rub a little toothpaste onto it, then buff with a soft cloth.

Plastic tubs: If you have any plastic containers that have absorbed the smell of food, leave them overnight in a solution of bicarbonate of soda (baking soda) and water. Rinse thoroughly and they should smell sweet and fresh.

Pots and pans: If some of your pots and pans need a bit of a facelift, fill them with water and add some white vinegar. Boil for several minutes and then rinse thoroughly.

Saucepans with copper bottoms can be cleaned by rubbing with tomato ketchup, then washing.

Refrigerator: All you need to clean your refrigerator is a cloth soaked in a strong solution of bicarbonate of soda (baking soda) and hot water. This will absorb any nasty odours and leave your refrigerator smelling fresh without contaminating any of the food.

Silver: Boil silver in a pan of water with a teaspoon of bicarbonate of soda (baking soda), a teaspoon of salt and a small piece of kitchen foil. If you need to get into any awkward places, use an old toothbrush and rub with a paste of bicarbonate of soda (baking soda) and water. Rinse thoroughly, then polish with a soft cloth.

Sinks: If you have a grubby porcelain sink, fill it with hot water, add a cupful of washing soda and leave it for two hours. After you drain it, you will find that any stains remaining will wipe away easily.

Stainless steel: Polish steel cutlery with old newspaper. Never be tempted to use bleach to remove stains from stainless-steel cutlery and sinks. Use a hot solution of detergent or a proprietary stainless-steel cleaner.

Teapots: Heavily stained china teapots can be cleaned by soaking overnight in water and washing powder.

To clean a teapot spout, pack it as tightly as possible with salt and leave it overnight before flushing it out.

Clean the inside of a metal teapot by filling it with water, dissolving a tablet for cleaning dentures in it and leaving overnight. Rinse well.

Vacuum flasks: Clean vacuum flasks by filling them with hot water, adding some rice and giving them a good shake.

Washing up: Soak dishes with starchy food such as potatoes or egg on them in cold water, not hot or warm: soak greasy ones in hot water with a little detergent squeezed into it.

Worktops: If you have a spot that needs a little abrasive action, say in the kitchen, then mix up some bicarbonate of soda (baking soda) with sufficient liquid soap to form a paste. Only mix a little at a time as this dries up very quickly.

For stubborn marks on your worktop, rub with a little lemon juice, then leave for a few minutes before rinsing off. This should help lift the mark.

For the living rooms

Candlesticks: If you put candlesticks, or other items covered in candle wax, in the freezer for a couple of hours, you can then peel off the hardened wax.

If you don't have time, wear rubber gloves and carefully run under very hot water.

Carpet deodorizer: Liberally sprinkle carpets with bicarbonate of soda (baking soda). Wait for 15 minutes and then simply vacuum up the powder.

CDs: If any of your CDs are losing clarity of sound, keep them in the freezer overnight. You will be astonished at how clear and clean they sound next time you play them.

Crystal: To make your crystal glasses sparkle like new, rinse them in a weak solution of white vinegar and warm water.

Decanters: The best way to clean a glass decanter is to fill it with finely chopped pieces of raw potato, add water and shake it well.

Furniture: A traditional wood polish can be made with a mixture of two parts olive oil to one part lemon juice. Apply sparingly, then buff it up using a soft cloth.

Leather furniture: Mix white vinegar and olive oil in the ratio 1:2 in an old jam jar and shake well. Pour a few drops onto a sponge and rub over the leather to remove any surface grime, then buff with a clean cloth.

Vases: If you have a stubborn stain on the bottom of a glass vase or cruet, fill it with hot water, drop in two effervescent indigestion tablets and when they've stopped fizzing, give the vase a shake and pour out the water.

For the bathroom
Grouting: If the grouting between your tiles is dirty, cut a lemon in half and wipe the cut side over the grouting.

Limescale: If you have hard water and the limescale builds up round your taps, soak some paper towels in neat vinegar and wrap around the base. Leave for at least an hour, then clean away the deposits.

Toilets: For a spotless bowl drop two Alka-Seltzer tablets into the water, wait 20 minutes, brush and flush!

Windows and mirrors: Mix 600ml (1 pint/2½ cups) of warm water with 225ml (8fl oz/1 cup) of white vinegar in a spray bottle. Wipe over with a sponge then buff to a shine with crumpled newspaper.
When cleaning windows, work vertically on one side and horizontally on the other. If you get streaks, you will be able to see which side they are on.

For the bedroom
Jewellery: Drop two effervescent indigestion tablets into a glass of water, drop in your jewellery for a minute or two and they'll come out like new.

Mattresses: Sprinkle bicarbonate of soda (baking soda) mixed with some crushed lavender flowers directly onto the mattress. Leave for two hours, then vacuum away the mixture to freshen the mattress.

Varnished woodwork: Wipe cold black tea over the surface, then buff with a soft, dry cloth.

PRACTICAL HINTS AND TIPS

Here's a selection of quick ideas that will help you resolve a stack of annoying inconveniences around the house.

In the kitchen

Can openers: Feeding a piece of kitchen paper through the jaws of a can opener will keep it clean.

Cast-iron pots: Don't scrub them too hard after use. Cast-iron pots need a thin coating of oil to stop them from rusting. It's much better simply to wipe them with kitchen paper after and before each use.

Dustpans: If you dampen your dustpan before you start sweeping up, the dust will stay where it should be – in the pan – and won't roll out.

Egg-stained cutlery: Don't pour away the water you've boiled eggs in. Use it to soak cutlery stained with the yolk.

Grill (broiler) pans: Biodegradable liners that trap excess fat are now available. This means you only need to wash the pan occasionally – but these are not suitable for grills (broilers) where the oven door is closed during use.

Melted plastic: If you leave a plastic bag near the cooker and it melts, turn the cooker off. When the mess has cooled, use nail-varnish remover to get rid of it.

Mop head: Sponge mop heads dry out then crack and break up if they are not used. Yours will last much longer if you wrap it in a plastic bag before you put it away after use.

Rubber gloves: If your gloves are difficult to get on, dust the inside with talcum powder. When you take them off, dry them over an empty milk bottle: if you leave them wet, the rubber will quickly perish.

Tumblers stuck together: If you left tumblers overnight, one inside the other, and they have become attached to each other so strongly they are reluctant to part, fill the top one with cold water and stand the bottom one in warm water. They will soon separate.

Tidy box: Keep a box under the stairs or in a convenient cupboard and put anything you find out of place in it. Once a month threaten to take the contents to a charity shop and you'll be surprised at how tidy the family becomes – especially if you actually do take everything to the local charity shop.

In the living room
Candles: Candles burn for longer if you keep them in the refrigerator before use.

Cobwebs: If you wipe a cobweb off a wall, it may be sticky and leave a stain. So always lift them off, using a vacuum cleaner or a broom with a cloth tied round the head.

Lost earring: If you lose an earring, a contact lens or similar small item at home, take the brush attachment off the vacuum cleaner and stretch the foot of one leg of a pair of tights over the end. Switch it on and sweep it over the carpet. It should pick up the missing item and the suction power will keep it firmly against the material.

Radiators: Clean old-fashioned radiators by hanging a damp towel between the columns and use a hairdryer to blow the dust onto it.

Scratches: Rubbing a Brazil nut on a scratch can disguise some surface damage in wooden furniture.

Silver: Silver tarnishes if it becomes damp when stored in a drawer. You can prevent this by putting a few pieces of chalk in with the silver to absorb any moisture.

Venetian blinds: The easiest way of cleaning these notoriously difficult-to-clean blinds is to soak a pair of fabric gloves in soapy water, put them on and slide each slat, one by one, between your fingers.

In the bathroom
Bathroom mirrors: Prevent bathroom mirrors from steaming up by spraying a thin coating of shaving cream onto the dry mirror and rubbing it with lint-free cloth until the cream disappears. You can also stop them fogging up by lighting candles when you have a bath or shower or running a couple of centimetres of cold water into the bath before adding the hot.

Missing plug: If you've lost your bath plug, a golf ball makes a good temporary substitute.

Curtains
Curtains fade more in the centre than the sides, so you may want to swap them to the opposite side of the window occasionally. If they are not hanging too well, slip a curtain rod through the bottom hem of each panel and leave it there for a day or two to straighten them out.

When you wash your curtains or have them dry-cleaned, wash the curtain rods as well and give them a coating of wax to make the curtains run more smoothly.

Before you send your curtains to be cleaned, mark the places where the hooks should be inserted with a blob of coloured nail varnish to make sure that you get them to hang properly when you get them back.

Dusting
Make your dusters last longer and work more efficiently by soaking new ones in a solution of one part glycerine and one part water and allowing them to dry thoroughly before use.

To dust fiddly ornaments, discard the duster and put an old sock over each hand. Using both hands will make the job very easy and cut the time taken.

LAUNDRY

Here are some tried-and-tested tips to make your life easier and help you save some money. They will help keep your clothes looking good for longer and all without costing the earth. Low-temperature programmes are the first choice for the energy-conscious; most fabrics are perfectly adequately washed at 30°C/86°F.

Preparation

Always check the manufacturer's washing instructions on the label of new garments so you can wash them on an appropriate programme.

Make sure any zips are done up before washing items such as trousers, as the teeth on metal zips can quickly wear holes in other items of clothing. Turn dark-coloured garments inside out to stop them fading.

If you put any small items, like a baby's socks, in a laundry bag, they will not get lost in the water outlet hose of the washing machine. Bras are also best in a laundry bag so that the hooks cannot snag other clothes. If you machine wash your more delicate clothes (hand washing is much kinder) they can also go in the laundry bag. Another option is to put them in a pillowcase and tie the end with a cord.

When washing new towels, leave them to soak for ten minutes in a bowl of water with a couple of tablespoons of white vinegar before putting them on a normal washing cycle. This will help the colours to set.

Improving results

Reduce static by adding a splash of white vinegar to the final rinse.

If you live in a hard-water area, add a dessertspoon of bicarbonate of soda (baking soda) to soften the water when hand-washing delicates.

If you find that your blacks are fading to greys, you can quickly restore their colour by adding some black coffee or strong black tea to the final rinsing water.

Washing and drying

Never wash elastic or elasticated garments in hot water or they will shrink. When you have washed them, don't wring or pull them – they'll stretch.

After washing, spin them for a short time, rolled up in towel to remove the excess moisture, then dry them flat – like wool.

If your knitted clothes come out of the wash covered with lots of little balls of fluff, stroke them very gently with a safety razor.

Dry silk, chiffon and crêpe garments between two towels to absorb the excess moisture then hang them on a hanger indoors to dry naturally. Never spin dry them.

Dry clothes outside if you can. Fresh air and sunlight have a natural deodorizing and purifying effect. It is much cheaper and more energy-efficient than using a tumble dryer and your clothes will last longer too.

If you are forced to use the tumble dryer during a spell of inclement weather, then make sure you always use dryer balls. You can easily make your own by rolling up a sheet of kitchen foil into a ball. Do not go out and leave a tumble dryer unattended.

Natural fabric conditioner

All you need for a natural fabric conditioner is some white vinegar. By adding a cup to the final rinse, it not only gets rid of any nasty smells and softens the clothes, it also helps eliminate any build-up of soap residue.

After you take your washing from the machine, keep used fabric softener sheets in a jar filled with a little liquid softener. When you are drying a load of clothes, take a sheet from the jar, squeeze out the excess moisture and pop it in the dryer.

NATURAL IRONING TIPS

Creased clothes: If you don't have a steam iron, dampen dry clothes with water from a plant spray before ironing them. If heavily creased, try laying a damp towel on the ironing board first and then place the clothes on top of the towel to iron. If you sponge a stubborn crease with some white vinegar and press it with a warm iron, it should disappear.

Delicate fabrics: Make sure you iron any delicate fabrics inside out to avoid getting shiny marks.

Dirty baseplate: If you have a sticky build-up on the plate of your iron, turn it to its highest setting and then pour a small amount of salt onto a sheet of greaseproof (waxed) paper. Run the hot iron back and forth over the paper until all the residue has gone.

Hems: If you need to let down a hem on an item of clothing, soak a clean cloth in a mixture of equal parts water and white vinegar. Lay the cloth over the flattened old hem, fold and iron over the cloth to help remove the fold.

Shirts: The easiest way to tackle a shirt is to iron the collar first, then the sleeves and finally the body.

Starching: If you want to starch something like a linen tablecloth or napkins, make your own mixture by adding 1 tablespoon of cornflour (corn starch) to 600ml (1 pint/2½ cups) of cold water in a spray bottle. Shake well each time you use it and spray the fabric lightly all over before ironing.

DEALING WITH STAINS

It's hardly going to ruin your life, but if a favourite item of clothing or furniture becomes stained, it's a nuisance and a waste. So here is how to deal with some common problems. Prewash stain-removal products are so much more efficient than in the past, that it makes no sense to list solutions that use things like methylated spirits, ammonia or borax – how many of us have those to hand? So the text includes just the more unusual and successful cleaning tips from the past.

First, a few basics:

- The quicker you act, the better the chance that the stain won't leave a permanent mark.

- Make sure the colour in the item won't run when the stain-remover is applied. On a piece of the fabric or area of the item that won't show, apply a little of the stain remover you are going to use and press gently between two pieces of cloth using a warm iron. If the stain remover marks the cloth, don't be tempted to tackle the stain yourself – take the garment to the dry cleaners.

- For any non-greasy stains on fabric, plunge the item into cold water while you work out what to do.

- Once you have treated the stain, wash as usual.

- If your efforts fail, ask the advice of your local dry cleaner or upholstery and carpet cleaner.

- Most stains – tea, felt-tip pen, wine, coffee, and so on – respond to a pre-soak in a solution of warm water and detergent.

Acrylic paint: Blot immediately, then wash with soap and cold water. If the paint has dried, scrape off as much as you can, then use paint remover – or even methylated spirits.

Beetroot (beet): Soak immediately in cold water and salt, then rub gently with detergent.

Bird droppings: Scrape off, sponge with salt water, then soak in warm detergent.

Blood: Soak in cold salt water, then rub gently to remove the stain.

Chewing gum: Put in the freezer until the gum is hard, then crack and scrape off. If the fabric is marked, rub with egg white or white vinegar before washing.

Clear adhesive: Remove with non-oily nail-varnish remover.

Coffee: Soak in hand-hot water and detergent.

Curry: Run under lukewarm water until it runs clear, then rub in a solution of equal parts glycerine and warm water and leave for 30 minutes.

Grease and fat: Scrape off any fat, sprinkle with talcum powder, leave for a few minutes, then brush off before washing at the highest temperature the fabric will stand.

Lipstick: Remove with dry-cleaning solvent, then wash.

Mascara: Rub with neat washing-up liquid, then wash as usual.

Mud: Allow to dry, then brush off as much as possible. Wash as usual.

Orange juice: Soak immediately in cold water, then wash as usual.

Pollen: Soak in cold water, then leave in the sunlight before washing.

Red wine: Sprinkle any highly coloured stains with salt, leave for half an hour to absorb the moisture, then vacuum or brush off.
   For carpets, blot with kitchen paper to remove as much of the liquid as possible, then wash with carpet shampoo.

Vomit: Squirt with a soda syphon and sponge off with a solution of bicarbonate of soda (baking soda).

In the fresh air

Gardening tips and enjoying the outdoors

if you are lucky enough to have your own garden, or any outdoor space such as a patio or balcony, it will have all kinds of advantages to your health and well-being if you use it well. Just sitting outside with the sun on your face will boost your vitamin D levels and can help you to relax and feel good. There's a natural peace about a garden; feeling the breeze on your face can act as a focus for meditation. This outdoor space may give you a bit more room to exercise and, of course, there's the chance to grow some of your own flowers or vegetables. If not, perhaps there is an open space or park nearby where you can (fresh air.

GARDENING BASICS

All you need to grow a few plants are soil, sun and water. Of course, that's only your starting point, but we are just going to look at a few basic gardening tips to get you going in a small way and in a small space. You don't need lots of equipment, acres of ground or vast knowledge. And you can apply these simple ideas to any outdoor space, including balconies, or even window boxes.

Assessing your options

First, draw a little plan of your space and find out which way your garden is facing. Watch the areas of the space during the day and jot down which parts get the sun at which time of day. Make a note of the type of soil you have: sticky clay that takes a shine when you rub your thumb over it, so light and sandy that it won't roll into a ball, or somewhere in between. If you are container gardening, get some all-purpose compost.

Depending on your space, plot out where you would like your flower beds, so that they get sun at least part of the day. Don't make the beds too large – you need to be able to reach all parts of each bed. Dig the soil over thoroughly, getting rid of any weeds, and dig in a little compost if you like.

Those with more space obviously have a bit more scope to divide the garden into separate beds or zones. You may want to edge your beds with bricks set into the soil at 45° to keep the edges neat, or perhaps broken tiles or wooden or plastic bed edging.

Pots and patios

You can grow all sorts of plants in pots on a patio or balcony, from tomatoes to sweet peas. Slightly larger pots are generally better as they allow enough root space for the plant, but do remember that they will be heavy when full of compost so position them before you fill them. You could also simply use grow-bags, which are very economical. When you water the pots, make sure it is not a nuisance to yourself or anyone below, if you are on a balcony. Plastic trays or even plates placed under your pots will help stop the water draining out and making a mess.

Before filling, put some broken pots, broken eggshells or gravel in the bottom of the pots for drainage. Alternatively, use old teabags to line the bottom of your plant pots and provide excellent drainage. Line the sides with bubble wrap to protect against frosts. Put the plant in the pot and fill with compost, pressing down gently to firm. Water thoroughly.

What to grow

Think about the plants you would like to grow, ideally suiting them to the space available and the type of soil you have. You also need to give some thought to their placement.

- Tall plants should go at the back.

- Aim for plants that flower in different seasons to give you colour all year if possible.

- Suit your plants to the type of soil.

- Don't buy plants that will quickly grow too big for the space.

- Look at the plants that are successful in your neighbours' gardens. Why not ask if you can have a root when they split any plants?

- Think about fragrance, too. Rosemary, lavender, roses, jasmine and honeysuckle are all beautifully scented.

- Go for healthy-looking specimens with strong leaves and bushy growth, and firm bulbs.

- Think about colours that go well together. You might have space for areas of one colour or you might prefer a random mix of colour.

- Include some evergreens to give structure and all-year colour.

- Coloured or variegated leaves can look very attractive, so include some of these if you like.

- You don't need to grow vegetables separately from flowers – they can all grow together. In fact, flowers attract pollinators which will help you get more fruit.

Beg or trade plants with friends and neighbours before you buy new plants. It's also a good way of breaking the ice with neighbours you don't know if you admire their gardens and ask for tips. If you do go to a garden centre, seek the advice of the assistants as they should be able to help you choose what's right for you.

Essential tools

You don't need a lot of tools to start a garden. If you paint the handles of the tools in bright colours, they are less likely to get lost if you forget to put them away. Apart from lawn tools, all you'll need for a small garden are:

- a trowel;
- gardening gloves;
- secateurs;
- a spade
- a fork.

Plant types

Plants grow in different ways and it is good to have a mixture in your garden.

Perennials: These carry on year after year. Some die back above ground in winter, such as sedums, while others are evergreen, such as rosemary. Many types are easy to grow as you don't have to do an awful lot with them.

Annuals: These plants germinate from seed, grow, flower and die in one season, leaving their seeds behind for next year, such as nigella.

Biennials: These have a two-year cycle, germinating and growing in one season, then flowering in the next, such as echiums, foxgloves and parsley.

You can also grow bulbs (daffodils, tulips), corms (gladioli, crocuses, freesias) and rhizomes (lily of the valley, irises, ferns, ginger) which flower and die back each year. Some can be successfully left in the ground; others are better if you lift them and store them in a cool, dry place. You can get plenty in an old pair of tights and hang them in the shed or a cupboard indoors. Plant bulbs in late autumn ready to flower the following spring. Keep tulips separate from narcissi (daffodils) as they don't grow well together.

The easiest way to get an 'instant' garden is to plant some perennials. Go to the garden centre or ask a friend if they will give you some plants to start you off.

You will also be able to plant perennials straight into the earth. Dig a hole comfortably larger than the plant's root ball, water the hole, then put the new plant in place, gently firm the soil around it and water it well. When planting roses, put a couple of banana skins at the bottom of the hole to add nutrients to the soil.

Growing plants from seeds and cuttings

If you are planting seeds, the packet will give full instructions for that plant. Some can be sown directly where they will grow, others need to be sown in seed trays or small pots filled with compost. You can make small pots out of a rolled tube of newspaper, twisting the bottom to keep in the soil. Egg boxes (cartons) are also useful. Sow the seeds in seed compost, then when the seedlings are sufficiently large, you can plant out the whole pot as the newspaper will decompose naturally. Where you have a clump of several seeds, gently tease out and discard the smaller ones – known as thinning out.

If you collect some of the seeds once the flowers have finished, you'll be able to start the cycle again next year. Tie a paper bag around the seed heads of maturing plants so the seeds drop into the bag when they ripen and dry. Old prescription bottles (non-childproof!) are ideal for storing seeds, or use film canisters (which can still be bought online). Make sure you label them otherwise you'll never remember which seeds they contain.

You can also propagate plants from cuttings. Cut off a piece of the growing end of a plant, dip the stem in rooting powder, and press into compost in a pot – again, newspaper pots are ideal. Put a few cuttings in each pot as they are rarely all successful and you can just pull them out if they don't take. If you are a keen flower arranger and use wet floral foam for your displays, you can reuse it to pot shrub cuttings. Insert the cuttings into the wet foam, and when the roots push through the foam, pot the seedlings up in the usual way, in suitable growing compost.

Another way to propagate is to divide clumps of perennial plants in autumn or spring, preferably on a cool day. Look for the best place to divide the plant where you will do least harm. Water the plant well before moving it. Cut back and shape large shrubs.

Keeping the soil fertile

You'll need to water your plants until they are established and if there is a spell of dry weather. Water in the cool of the morning or evening so that the plants have a chance to absorb the water and the water droplets on the leaves are not magnified by the sun and burn the leaves.

Keep the garden tidy by cutting the grass regularly and digging over the earth to keep it free of weeds. Cut hedges once or twice a year after flowering. Trim off flower heads once they have died and cut back plants when they finish their season and go brown. Trim shrubs after flowering.

Check with your local garden centre about feeding the soil with nutrients. One of the best ways is to have your own compost heap where you can throw all your chopped trimmings, plants that have died back, weeds and so on. You can also add your vegetable peelings from the kitchen and ashes from a wood-burning stove, if you have one. Chop everything that goes in the bin, mix it up, and just wait for the rich, brown compost to form so you can spread it over the garden.

The most convenient compost containers have a removable front panel to allow easy access. This makes regular turning easier and also makes the well-rotted compost more accessible when you want to remove some of it to spread in the garden. You can also buy revolving composters, or tumblers, to simply the job of turning the contents.

If you have an open compost heap, cover it with a tarpaulin or a piece of old carpet to help it warm up and naturally break down. After about three months, remove the compost and put it all back. This process adds air to the mixture and helps it rot even faster. Speed it up even more by adding some banana skins or commercial compost accelerator.

- You can compost non-glossy shredded paper, uncooked vegetable trimmings and peelings, cooked vegetables (if simply steamed or boiled), tea bags, coffee grounds (and coffee filters), annual weeds, old bedding plants, soft hedge clippings, dead leaves, and lawn mowings.

- You should not try to compost woody material such as thick prunings, thick stems (unless shredded first), synthetic fabrics, food scraps, meat or bones, diseased plant material, weeds with seed heads, perennial roots, or dog or cat faeces.

You might want to erect a screen in front of the compost bin: grow climbers, such as clematis, up some bamboo poles to hide it, or make a wigwam for sweet peas or runner beans – useful as well as practical.

Making life easy with mulch

A good mulch will protect plants in winter and stop the spread of weeds. A mulch is a protective layer applied to the surface of the ground around your plants to help retain nutrients and moisture and stop weeds getting established. Old carpets make great mulch. Cut a square or circle of carpet slightly larger than the root system of a plant and make a slit in it to enable you to put the carpet round the plant, making sure you have a nice gap around the plant stem so you don't damage it. When you're done, cover the carpet with a thin layer of chipped bark or soil.

A layer of old newspaper several sheets thick, anchored with rock, is another terrific mulch. It's cheap, it conserves water and it's bio-degradable. But only use the black and white section – coloured ink may contain lead and damage the plants.

Frost protection

Your mulch will help hold heat in the soil, but if you know a frost is coming you can give your tender plants additional protection. A light covering of straw, dead bracken or leaves will help. You could also cut off the bottom section of a lemonade bottle and press it into the ground over tender plants that are sprouting early to act like a mini greenhouse and protect them from frost damage.

Your own herb garden

Fresh herbs are much better than dried ones, more healthy for flavouring food than salt, fragrant, easy to grow and often available throughout the year. Lots of our favourite herbs – basil, oregano, rosemary, sage, thyme, and more – love Mediterranean conditions. They tolerate relatively poor soil, but they do love sunshine so a south-facing, well-drained slope is ideal, or you can grow them in pots on your patio.

Evergreens: Bay, rosemary, rue, sage, thyme. Evergreen perennials look attractive all year round.

Herbaceous: Chives, marjoram, mint, oregano, savory, tarragon. These are perennials that die back in the winter, so cut them down and tidy up at the end of summer. Mint tends to be invasive so keep it in a pot, or cut the base off the pot of mint and plant the whole thing in the ground. This should stop it taking over your herb bed.

Annuals: Basil, chervil, coriander and dill grow from seed every season.

Biennials: Plant parsley to mature the following year.

HOME-GROWN VEG

It is wonderful to grow your own vegetables, and even if you don't get very many, it's a great sense of achievement as you bite into your own produce.

If you have a vegetable garden, rotate your crops so that the soil is not depleted by growing the same crops in the same place each year, and dig in plenty of compost between crops.

Depending on where you are and how the weather varies, you will need to adapt this basic guide to suit your own circumstances.

Early spring

- As the soil begins to warm up, tidy off dead stems and leaves and gently dig over the soil.

- Keep seed potatoes in a dry, dark place so that they begin to sprout. Plant them out in spring, for early varieties, or late spring for maincrop varieties.

- Plant onion sets about 30cm (12in) apart on a dry day.

- Other vegetables that can be planted are Jerusalem artichoke tubers and asparagus.

- Harvest any winter root vegetables, such as Brussels sprouts, cauliflowers, leeks and parsnips, kale and swede (rutabaga).

- Soak runner-bean seeds in a bowl of hot water. Discard those that float to the top, then soak the remainder for 24 hours before planting.

Mid spring

- Plant out early potatoes in a trench about 20cm (8in) deep and 30cm (12in) apart.

- Plant strawberries. It is a good idea to pinch out the flowers in the first year because this will give the plants added strength and give you an improved crop the following year. Replace plants every three or four years. They do well in containers on a patio.

- Other things you can sow now are beetroot (beet), peas, broad (fava) beans, broccoli, Brussels sprouts, cabbage, cauliflower, chard, kale, kohlrabi, leeks, lettuce, radishes, rocket (arugula) and spinach .

Late spring

- There are many things to sow now: beetroot (beet), broccoli, cabbage, cauliflower, chicory (endive), French beans, kale, kohlrabi, peas, radishes, runner beans, swede (rutabaga), salad leaves (in succession), spring onions (scallions) and turnips.

- You can also plant out aubergine (eggplant), (bell) peppers, Brussels sprouts, celeriac (celery root), celery, cucumber, leeks, summer cabbage and tomatoes.

- You may well have hardy lettuce, fast-growing radishes, and spring onion (scallions) ready for harvesting.

- Established asparagus beds may also be starting to crop.

- Provide support once your runner beans get to 20cm (8in) high.

Early summer

- There are plenty of things you can begin to sow this month, planting some now and some in a few weeks to give you a succession of crops: beetroot (beet), carrots, cauliflower, chicory (endive), courgettes (zucchini), cucumbers, French and runner beans, kohlrabi, marrows, maincrop peas, squash, swede (rutabaga), sweetcorn and turnips.

- You can now plant out brassicas such as Brussels sprouts and, if you haven't already done so, broccoli and summer cabbage.

- Tumbling tomatoes are easy to grow in pots or grow bags as they do not grow tall and will not require pinching out.

- Watch out for the eggs of butterflies on the undersides of brassicas as they will hatch into caterpillars which can soon make a meal of your crop.

- Salad crops should be ready to harvest – early carrots, lettuce, radishes, spring onions (scallions) and summer cabbage. Early potatoes should be ready this month, as well as beetroot (beet), summer spinach and young turnips.

Mid-summer

- Water your crops regularly and put a layer of organic mulch on the surface of the vegetable bed to keep the moisture in. Don't waste your cold tea – plants thrive on it.

- There are still a few crops you can sow this month: beetroot (beet), spring cabbage, carrots, chicory (endive), kohlrabi, lettuce, peas, French beans, and radishes.

- Plant out your leeks in 15cm (6in) deep holes and water well.

- There should be plenty to pick this month: French and runner beans, beetroot (beet), cabbage, cauliflower and broccoli, carrots, celery, courgettes (zucchini), cucumbers, kale, kohlrabi, lettuce, onions, spring onions (scallions), peas, early potatoes, radishes, spinach, tomatoes and turnips. When harvesting your potatoes, make sure you dig the ground well to ensure you have removed all the tubers.

- Keep on top of aphids (particularly on the tips of broad (fava) beans) by washing them off the plants with a strong jet of water, or spray with a solution of liquid soap and water. This will not damage the plants and hopefully will reduce the numbers. I would advise planting some African marigolds among your vegetables as they are well known to be the perfect companion plant. They exude chemicals from their roots that help to repel pests from neighbouring plants.

- Pour boiling water over weeds and sprinkle dandelions with salt to get rid of them.

Late summer

- You can still sow kohlrabi, winter lettuce, radishes, spinach, spring cabbage, spring onions (scallions) (winter hardy), and turnips.

- Cauliflowers, kale, and Savoy cabbages can all be planted out this month.

- Again, there should be plenty for the kitchen: lettuce, onions, spring onions (scallions) peas, early maincrop potatoes, radishes, spinach, tomatoes, turnips, French beans, runner beans, cabbages, carrots, cauliflower, celery, courgettes (zucchini), cucumbers, kale and kohlrabi.

- If your neighbour's weeds are creeping under the fence into your garden, dig a trench 30cm (12in) deep on your side of the fence and line it with heavy-duty polythene, then replace the soil.

Early autumn

- There is not much to sow at this time of year except perhaps a winter lettuce for spring harvest.

- You can plant out spring cabbages and Japanese onions sets can go in for an early harvest.

- There are still plenty of crops to harvest, including beetroot (beet), cabbages, carrots, cauliflowers, courgettes (zucchini), cucumbers, globe artichokes, kale, kohlrabi, lettuce, leeks, marrows, onions, squashes, radishes, spring onions (scallions), spinach, sweetcorn, tomatoes and turnips.

- Maincrop potatoes should be ready for harvesting now. Dig them up early in the day and leave them in the sunlight for a day so that the skins harden off before storing. That way there is less risk of damage. Do not put any damaged potatoes in your sacks as they will quickly rot and damage the rest of the potatoes.

Mid-autumn

- Start collecting leaves to make leaf mould. Build yourself a cage by driving four stakes into the ground and stapling some chicken wire around them. Just throw the leaves in there and leave for a year or more. A good leaf mould makes an excellent seed compost or, if only partially rotted, it can be used as a mulch or soil improver.

- Split and plant rhubarb crowns.

- Sow hardy winter lettuce, which will give you some salad leaves whatever the weather.

- Lift the last maincrop potatoes and carrots.

- Leave the parsnips in the ground as the flavour improves after a frost.

- Cabbages should come up now and they will keep well if you have a shed that is sheltered from frost.

- If you have any green tomatoes left on your tomato plants, you may as well pick them now before they are destroyed by frost. You can ripen them indoors or make green tomato chutney.

Late autumn

- This is the time to plant garlic as it actually benefits from the cold weather.

- Bring in winter cabbages, cauliflowers and Brussels sprouts, and any remaining carrots.

- Harvest leeks as you need them and leave the rest in the ground.

- Other things that could still be available are celery, celeriac, kale, kohlrabi, turnips, swede (rutabaga) and spinach. Jerusalem artichokes will also be ready.

- Parsnips can stay in the ground until needed – in fact, you won't be able to pull them out if the ground is frozen.

Winter

Through the winter months, you can virtually put your feet up and wait for spring when the process will start all over again. There will be just a few things you can still harvest such as Brussels sprouts and parsnips, but most vegetables require the warmer months. Use the time to have a good tidy up of the garden.

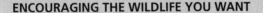

ENCOURAGING THE WILDLIFE YOU WANT

There are many animals that have a place even in a small garden.

Birds

It is lovely to watch the birds in the garden. During the cold winter months, birds look for extra food to supplement their diet. You can help them out by putting a bird table in your garden and giving them scraps from your kitchen along with peanuts and birdseed. This should encourage the birds to stay in your garden even when the weather gets warmer.

Don't give bread to birds when they are feeding their young as the nestlings find it hard to digest.

Place some nest boxes in secluded places in your garden to encourage birds to breed. Ideally, place a nest box so it is facingto avoid too much direct sun or prevailing winds. You can also buy nest boxes which are specifically designed for bats.

Hedgerows

Hedgerows and shrubs provide perfect shelter and nesting places for birds. They also offer shelter to other animals, such as mice. Try to include some evergreen shrubs or hedges in your garden to provide year-round protection against the elements for these creatures.

Pond

A pond encourages birds, insects, mammals and amphibians to your garden. Make sure your pond has gently sloping sides to allow creatures to climb in and out, as well as deeper areas and also some stones to allow animals to sit and absorb the sunlight. You can make your pond look attractive by including aquatic plants such as water lilies.

Compost heaps, log piles and rockeries

These are great for attracting all kinds of insects as well as slow worms (which will eat your slugs and snails), and you might find that a hedgehog will choose to hibernate in the warmth of the compost.

It is a good idea to leave some old logs lying in a corner of the garden as the rotting wood makes a perfect habitat for all kinds of insects and invertebrates.

Rockeries and dry-stone walls can give shelter to frogs, toads and newts as they are attracted by the damp, dark area beneath the stones.

Nectar-rich flowers

Make sure you plant plenty of flowers that are rich in nectar to encourage bees, butterflies and moths. These include: monkshood, bugle, foxgloves, hollyhocks, anemones, aubrieta, borage, campanula, wallflowers, poppies, geraniums, gypsophila, sunflowers, hellebores, bluebells, candytuft, honeysuckle, poached-egg plant, honesty, forget-me-not, rhododendrons, clover, verbena and zinnias.

DETERRING THE WILDLIFE YOU DON'T WANT

Although chemicals may help you get rid of unwanted pests, these chemicals can have a harmful effect on the beneficial wildlife too. Try to find natural ways of dealing with pests that will not harm the environment.

Ants

Next time you see columns of ants on the move, put copper wire or copper coins in their way. Weirdly enough, ants will not cross copper.

Birds

While they are great to watch, you don't want the birds on your crops. Keep them off crops by hanging CDs around to spin in the wind, or if you can get hold of some old cassette tapes at a car-boot (yard) sale, stretch the tape between posts around the vegetables. The tape vibrates in the breeze and makes a sound that deters birds.

When your marrows are starting to ripen, keep them from the attention of birds by wrapping them in old tights or stockings. Pull the leg over one end of each marrow and tie it securely at the other.

Cats

Cats hate the smell of oranges, so if you sprinkle some finely chopped orange peel around your garden, they should avoid it. They also don't like getting their paws prickled, so if you push some rose prunings or holly leaves into the soil, they will stay away.

Another trick is to scatter mothballs on the flowerbeds.

Dogs

Discourage dogs from crawling under your fence by planting pyracantha or a similar prickly shrub at their entry points.

Earwigs

If these garden pests are making a meal of your young plants, roll up some damp newspaper and leave it near where the bugs have been at work. Next morning it will be full of them, and you can then dispose of them.

Greenfly (plant lice)

If greenfly (plant lice) are getting at your pot plants and hanging baskets, next time you plant them, add a French marigold. The pesky insects don't like marigolds at all and will give the containers a wide berth.

If they have been feasting on your roses, plant a clove of garlic at the base of each rose bush.

Leatherjackets

If you see starlings feasting on your lawn, you could well have leatherjackets, the larvae of the crane fly, in the grass. Get rid of them by watering the lawn and covering it with black polythene. Next morning, when you roll the polythene back, you should find that the grubs have stuck to it.

Mice and other little pests

Protect your saplings from the unwanted attentions of mice, rabbits and other pests by wrapping the trunks in fibreglass insulation, and keeping it there until the young tree is well established.

If you use nets to protect your vegetables and fruits, check them regularly to ensure that no birds or small mammals have become trapped in them. And if they are, put on a pair of stout gloves before trying to free them. A panicky bird can give you a nasty peck and many small mammals have very sharp teeth. Be gentle, though, because these creatures are delicate.

Slugs and snails
Look out for slugs wherever the conditions are damp. Bury a yogurt pot up to the top and fill with beer, or use a half coconut shell. Slugs will go for a drink and drown. You can also bake old eggshells in the oven for a few minutes to harden them, then crush them and sprinkle them around the plants. A sprinkling of bran around seedlings also deters slugs, as do prickly leaves like holly.

If you like hostas and cultivate them on your patio or conservatory, make sure that they don't suffer from the unwelcome attention of slugs by smearing petroleum jelly all the way round the pot, 10cm (4in) down from the rim.

Squirrels
To stop squirrels and birds attacking your fruit before you have a chance to pick it, buy some cheap aluminium plates, puncture a hole in them and tie them close together to the lower branches of the trees. It may look odd, but as the plates clang in the breeze, the scavengers will be scared off. You could do the same with CDs.

Whitefly
Whitefly hate garlic and will give even the merest whiff of it a wide berth, so try companion planting of your cabbages with garlic and onions, or use a garlic spray.

DIY

How to avoid stressing about simple home improvements

Employing a professional plumber, decorator or other worker is expensive, and while it is important to look around locally and find the most talented individuals for major projects that need expert knowledge, you'll find it will reduce your stress levels if you can make simple home repairs and improvements yourself to avoid having to put up with something that is broken or not working properly, or to watch it get worse and worse until you have to hire a specialist at an even greater cost.

I could also mention the refrain that has popped up all through the book: prevention is better than cure. Keep your tools clean, your appliances well maintained and regularly serviced, your home tidy and organized. Then repairs will be minimized.

BASIC TOOL KIT

You don't need a huge, fancy toolkit, but a few basics will certainly come in handy before long. Always make sure your tool kit is stored where it is easily accessible to you but safe from children. And do put things in their right place so you know where to find them next time.

Drill: An electric drill and set of bits is vastly easier than a hand drill. You only need a basic model to start out.

Filler: A tube of ready-mixed all-purpose filler.

Filling knife: A flat-bladed knife for smoothing and filling.

Hammer: A medium-sized claw hammer is the most useful type.

High-strength grab adhesive: Use this instead of nails or screws but note that whatever you stick in place will be very difficult to remove should you ever want to.

Masking tape: To mask areas before painting to give a clean edge. Use low-tack varieties and remove it as soon as possible to prevent leaving marks or residue.

Measuring tape: Retractable.

Nails and screws: An assortment.

Pencil: It is always best to mark where you want a shelf or other item to go, and to mark screw-hole positions and so on.

Pliers: A small pair of pointed-nose pliers should do.

Rawl plugs (screw anchors): Assorted sizes for inserting into a hole in the wall before a screw.

Sandpaper (glasspaper): Medium grade. Add other grades to your stash as and when you need them.

Screwdriver: If you don't use one frequently, the best type to buy is one with interchangeable heads, including both flat and cross heads in various sizes. If you find using one a strain, or have a big job to do such as putting together a large flat-pack item, consider buying a power screwdriver or a cordless drill that doubles up as a power screwdriver.

Silicone spray: Lubricant spray, such as WD40.

Spirit level: If you are likely to be putting up shelves, pictures, and so on.

Wire-cutters: Invaluable when it comes to changing a plug, snipping wire for craft projects or other household and gardening jobs.

DIY TIPS AND TECHNIQUES

Sometimes, it's the little things that your parents told you that make the DIY process easier. Run through these tips and gain some useful experience in minutes that would otherwise take you years.

Around the house

Bath sealant: When using sealant around a bath or sink, fill the bath with water first – this stops the bath breaking away from the sealant later with the extra weight.

Broken china: Next time you are gluing broken china, smear some petroleum jelly round the edges of the break. It stops any surplus glue that oozes out from setting. When you have finished, simply wipe the jelly off with a damp cloth.

Cleaning hands: Try rubbing a little petroleum jelly on your hands before you start decorating. It seals the pores and makes the paint slide off more easily.

Drawer fronts loose: Scrape off the old glue with a sharp knife and spread new PVA wood glue on the surfaces. Hold the two pieces together using a clamp until the glue has set.

Drawers sticking: If a drawer becomes stuck or the handle comes off and you can't get it back on without opening the drawer, try opening it with a rubber plunger. It should be strong enough to get the drawer open and won't leave a permanent mark on the wood.

   If a drawer doesn't open and close easily, rub a bar of soap or a candle along the runners or in the runner channels to smooth out the movement.

Glue: Less is best. You can always put more onto something that isn't sticking properly, but it can be difficult to get rid of the excess if you put too much on to start with.

Keys sticking: If your house or car keys are sticky, work a lead pencil all over them or rub them with soap, then gently work the key in the lock. You can also spray the lock with silicone spray.

Ladder safety: When climbing up and down a ladder, always use two hands and always face the ladder. Keep your tools in your belt or pocket, or haul them up and down in a bucket with a rope attached to the handle, long enough to stretch from the top of the ladder to the ground with some to spare. Carry a whistle or mobile phone just in case. Better still, ask someone to stand at the bottom of the ladder, keeping it steady.

Loft insulation: When you are insulating your loft, always work from the eaves towards the middle. That way, when you need to cut to fit (as you are sure to) you can work in the area with the most headroom.

Measuring round: If you need to measure a round object, take a piece of string and wrap it around the object, marking where both ends meet. Lay the piece of string out flat on a table and then measure it with a tape measure or rule.

Putting up pictures: If you have several pictures to hang, lay them out on the floor to see how they relate to one another or cut out paper shapes the size of each picture and Blu-tack them to the wall in likely positions. Mark the position for the hanging screws; larger pictures will need two screws to hold their weight. Drill holes, press in rawl plugs (screw anchors), then screw in the screws until tight but just protruding.

Rawl plugs or tile spacers: Burnt matches make ideal substitutes.

Restoring faded wood: Mix one part linseed oil with four parts of white spirit, wipe on and leave for a few minutes, then take off the old wax with another cloth. Once the surface is dry and clean, give it a couple of coats of polish and buff up to a shine.

Rusted bolts: Try pouring some fizzy drink over a bolt that is reluctant to come undone.

Saw protectors: Use a piece of polystyrene packing to protect your saw blades or other sharp tools in storage.

Self-sticking hooks: Coat the sticky side with clear nail varnish before putting them in place – somehow they're never as sticky as you think they are going to be!

Squeaky floorboards: Try sprinkling talcum powder or French chalk around the joints to stop floorboards from squeaking.

Vinyl floor tiles: If one or two vinyl floor tiles need replacing, cover with an old dish towel and then warm up with an iron. This softens the adhesive underneath the tiles and makes it easier to prise them off. Scrape the old adhesive from the floor and check the fit of the replacement tiles. Warm the new tiles with an iron, as before, then spread fresh adhesive on the floor, lay the new tiles in place and weigh down with bricks or a suitably heavy object until the adhesive is dry.

Zips (zippers): Rub a sticking zip with a pencil or the edge of a bar of soap so it glides more easily. If the tab comes off, fix a small paperclip through the hole and wind suitably coloured thread round it.

Power and utilities

Bleeding radiators: If your radiators are hot at the bottom and cold at the top, there is air in the system that needs to be bled out. Hold an old towel under the valve at the top of the radiator and insert a radiator key. Turn the key slowly until the air starts to hiss out. The water will rise up the radiator and start to splutter out of the valve. As soon as that happens, tighten the valve.

Blocked drains: Try to avoid blocked drains by not putting bits of food waste or fat down them. If one does become blocked, place a plunger totally over the plughole and gently push it up and down to create a vacuum and dislodge the blockage.

Never put tea leaves down the sink – they clog it up. Some people believe that coffee grounds help keep drain pipes free of grease but, like tea leaves, these can cause a blockage, so always dispose of them with other food waste rather than tipping them down the sink.

Keep your external drains clear by dissolving washing soda in boiling water and pouring it down.

Blocked sinks: Before calling the plumber, crumble three effervescent indigestion tablets and put them down the drain followed by a cup of white vinegar. Wait for a few minutes then run the hot water. Alternatively, try using a plunger. If you have plastic sink fittings you may be able to unscrew the U-shaped trap under the sink and unblock it from there, but don't forget to put a bowl under it before setting to work, and make sure you put the trap back on securely afterwards. If a ring or other important item goes down the plughole, you may well find it in the trap.

Frozen pipes: If your pipes are frozen, turn the water off at the stopcock immediately and open all the taps. When you identify the frozen section, use a hair drier set on cool to begin to defrost it. Never use boiling water, propane torches of any kind of naked flame as excessive heating can cause a pipe to explode.

Fuses: The fuse is the deliberate weakest link in an electric circuit, so if anything goes wrong, it blows the fuse instead of creating more serious problems.

If the fuse blows in a plug, lever out the fuse cartridge in the centre of the plug, replace it with one of the same rating and securely return it to the plug. On older plugs, undo the central screw on the plug and replace the fuse with one of the same rating, then screw the plug back together.

Houses should have a modern fuse box so if anything goes wrong with an electric circuit, one lever will flip up. Once you have established the problem – it may be a light bulb has blown, for example – simply return the lever to the 'on' position to restore the circuit.

Most appliances come with a sealed plug but it is a good idea to know plug wiring in case you ever need to change a plug.
There are three wires:

- Neutral (N): blue or black (white for USA).

- Live (L): brown or red (black, red or blue for USA).

- Earth (E): green and yellow or green.

Each wire should go to the relevant pin on the plug. Colours vary in different countries so check the colour codes before you start.

Unscrew and remove the plug cover. If a wire has worked itself loose from the terminal, undo the screw on the top of the terminal, push the wire inside and tighten the screw down again to hold it tight. There should also be a cable grip where the cable enters the plug, which should be screwed down to hold the cable tight and stop any wires working loose again.

Nailing and drilling

Nailing: Try not to nail in a straight line along the grain as it can cause the wood to split.

Nailing thick and thin wood: Always nail through the thinner piece into the thicker and, if possible, use nails that are three times longer than the thinner piece.

Concealing nailheads: Chisel a small shaving parallel to the wood grain, at the point where the nail is to be hammered in, leaving the end of the shaving attached to the surface. Once the nail is in, fix the shaving back in place with a suitable adhesive.

Removing nails: When you are using a claw hammer to remove a nail from a piece of wood, protect the surface by slipping a thin piece of scrap wood or rubber under the hammer head so that you don't scratch or dent the wood.

Drill bits: Spray your drill bits with a silicone spray before you use them and they will stay sharper longer and be less likely to break.

Drilling: Never drill or nail directly above, below or level with a power socket or switch as cables are always laid at right angles so you could drill through them.

To avoid a mess, stick an open envelope to the wall beneath the hole to catch the dust. Alternatively, vacuum as you drill.

Drilling ceilings: if you are drilling into a ceiling, keep the dust from raining into your eyes by making a collar from the bottom of an old yoghurt pot and drilling though it.

Drilling tiles: Stick a piece of masking tape onto the tile first to prevent the drill bit from slipping.

Drilling a specific depth: Place a piece of masking tape around the drill bit at the required depth. As soon as the drill reaches the tape, you know you have reached the desired depth.

Drilling wood: Rest the piece you are drilling on a piece of scrap wood. It stops the wood splitting when it breaks through the other side.

Hammering and screwing

Hammering: Always hold the hammer as far from the head as possible and once the nail is firmly in, swing the hammer from your elbow. This will exert the maximum energy on the nail.

Hold the nail with a clothes peg or the teeth of a comb to avoid hitting your finger or thumb.

Loose screws: To sort out any annoyingly loose screws, remove each wobbly screw, wedge a piece of matchstick into the hole and screw the offender back in. The match should hold it tightly in place.

Screwdriver sizes: Try to ensure that the tip of the screwdriver you plan to use is as close as possible to the width and length of the slot in the screw. If the tip is too narrow, you may damage the slit, making it hard to take the screw out should you ever need to. If it's too wide, the screwdriver may slip and scratch the wood.

Slippery screws: To make screws easier to remove at a later date, rub some soap over the thread before screwing them in. If you are screwing into wood, first dip screws in some petroleum jelly to make life easier. You can also put a dab of clear nail varnish under the screw head before screwing it tight.

Screwing into hard-to-reach places: Before you start, push the screw through a slit of masking tape with the adhesive side up, put the screwdriver in the screw's slit and fold the tape up, sticking the sides together to hold the screw in position on the screwdriver. Just pull off the tape when you're done.

Storing nails and screws: Keep nails and screws in jars and fix the lids to the underside of shelves so they don't waste space.

Tight screws: If a screw is proving too tight to get out, try heating the tip of your screwdriver.

Filling and painting

Holes to fill: All-purpose filler is quick drying and easy to sand. Deeper holes should be stuffed with newspaper before filling over the top.

Paint: When you re-use old paint, strain it through the feet end of an old pair of tights to filter out any impurities.

Paint stirrer: A wire coat hanger makes a useful paint stirrer – much better than the handle of an old spoon or piece of wood.

Paint tray: Line paint trays with kitchen foil before use, then you can simply throw away the foil when the job is finished. Cover your paint tray or brushes completely with a sealed plastic bag between painting sessions.

Wood filler: Repairs will be much less conspicuous if you mix a little instant coffee powder into the wood filler.

Outdoor preparation and maintenance

Cold weather: Weather patterns are vastly different throughout the regions of the world so you will be aware of the prevailing conditions in your area and the chances of severe weather. However bad it is likely to be, being prepared will make all the difference.

If snow is forecast, take a shovel and keep it indoors or in the porch. That way, if the snow does fall and you have to clear the path, you won't have to tread through thick snow to get to where you usually keep your shovels.

You might also like to have some de-icer ready, and some newspaper to cover the windows of the car. A sack of rock salt is useful to sprinkle on the drive, especially if it is steep.

Flood risk: If you live in an area liable to flooding, you will know the drill. You may have a flood gate and will almost certainly be given sandbags. Get these in place in advance.

Guttering: Check if your gutters are flowing freely by running water along them from a garden hose. Clear the gutters once a year and mend any sections that are dripping. If leaves are a constant problem, it is worth investing in gutter covers or inserts to keep out the debris.

DECORATING

Start with a relatively simple project and you should find you can enjoy changing the colour schemes in your home and brightening up the paintwork. It is fun thinking about what you are going to change. Start by deciding what will remain as that gives you the basis for the scheme. Then decide on the main items, followed by the smaller accents. Have all your materials ready.

If you are buying wallpaper, make sure you have enough and make allowance for pattern matching and the odd mishap.

Preparation

Preparation is key. Clear the room as much as possible and cover up any furniture left behind with dust cloths – old shower curtains are ideal.

- Rub down the walls and make sure they are smooth. Fill and rub down any holes.

- Rub down all the paintwork with sandpaper (glasspaper) wrapped around a small block of wood about the size of a large bar of soap, then vacuum and wash down the surfaces to get rid of as much dust as you can.

- If you are painting skirting boards, use masking tape all round the edge of the carpet to protect it. If you are painting windows, do the same on the glass. Alternatively, keep the glass free of paint by covering it with damp strips of newspaper, which will stay in place long enough for you to paint the frame and then easily peel off.

- Where there are switches or wall fittings, either mask them, unscrew them slightly from the wall so you can paint behind them, or cover each one with a polythene bag and secure it with an elastic band.

- If there is any damp or mildew on the walls, apply a little household bleach and clean thoroughly before painting.

- You will get a better finish if you strip off wallpaper and line the walls with lining paper. However, if you are painting wallpaper, paint a sample patch in an unseen part of the room (above the skirting board behind the door, or under the window beneath the curtain) so that you can check any show-through.

Painting

Avoid painting in strong sunlight as the paint will dry too quickly and you may end up with an uneven result. That applies particularly to painting outside, and it is also better not to start exterior painting until the dew has dried and to finish in the evening before any dampness sets in.

- Start with the emulsion and work your way round the room: ceilings, walls, then doors and windows. Try to work uninterrupted for three or four hours at a stretch. This allows you to work in consistent light and you should be able to get the first coat on in an average-size room in that time.

- If you don't like the smell of paint, put half an onion, cut-side up, on a plate in the room to help dissipate the smell.

- Move on to the gloss paint. If the job is going to take more than a day, wrap your brush tightly in cling film (plastic wrap) overnight so that it doesn't dry out.

- If you do get paint on the windows and it's still fresh, wash it off with a solution of three parts warm water to one part vinegar. If it has hardened, you'll have to scrape it off carefully using a single-edged razor blade.

- Use special non-metallic paint for painting radiators. Metallic paints absorb heat so radiators painted with it will not be as warm, and your heating bill may rise.

- If you have a very fiddly job – such as painting railings – consider using a spray paint. Mask off the area, put some cardboard behind and you will do the job much more quickly.

- If you are painting stairs, paint alternate treads, then go back and paint the others when the first lot are dry so you can still go up and down the stairs two at a time.

Wallpapering

- Prime the walls with a pre-wallpaper primer or thin wallpaper paste. Leave to dry for 24 hours. Decide where you are going to paste your first strip. It should be in the middle of a wall and placed so that when you get to the corners, the corner is positioned near the centre of the roll – don't have a strip finishing in a corner.

- Hang a plumb line from the ceiling where you are going to paste your first strip and mark a vertical pencil line. Measure and cut your first strip the height of the wall plus 7.5cm (3in). Paste it, then carefully concertina fold it, without creasing the paper. You may find that putting the paste in a paint tray and applying it with a roller helps it go on more evenly than with a brush.

- Lift the paper and brush it into position, aligned with your vertical mark, with a slight overlap on the ceiling and skirting board. Wipe off any excess paste with a clean cloth.

- Gently push into the top and bottom edges using a straight edge, and cut off the excess. Brush back into position and wipe off any excess paste.

- Match the pattern on your next strip, cut and paste, then gently brush into position on the wall, sliding it next to the first piece so they butt together perfectly and don't overlap.

- To paper round switches or sockets, lay the strip of paper as normal, then use a sharp blade to cut a cross over the top of the switch. Using the brush, push the paper round the edges and then trim using a sharp blade.

- For future reference, use a permanent marker on the top of the door to write the number of rolls of wallpaper needed for the room.

- Drying wallpaper can look a bit lumpy but it will flatten as the paste dries. If a few bubbles remain that have no paste behind them, inject some more paste into the bubble with a syringe and smooth it flat.

- Clean the room thoroughly and return the furniture to its place.

SAFETY IN THE HOME

Especially when you are decorating, it is a good time to check up on safety issues in the house and make sure they are up to date. Some of these points apply only when you have young children in the house.

Safety for everyone

- Check your smoke alarms, test them and replace the batteries, if necessary.

- Make sure that hallways, stairs and all exits are clearly lit and free of any obstructions. Don't leave things on the stairs.

- Use mats with non-slip backing or place a sheet of non-slip mesh under rugs on hard floors.

- Use a non-slip bath mat.

- Put grab bars on either side of the bath or in the shower.

- Check that you have safety locks on upstairs windows.

- Shorten cords on window blinds.

- When pans are on the hob, turn them so the handles are facing to the sides, not over the heat or protruding over the edge of the worktop.

Child safety

- Cover any electrical sockets with childproof covers.

- Keep cleaning products and medications locked away.

- Use child-safety gates on stairs, as appropriate.

- Never leave a child unattended in the kitchen.

- Keep sharp utensils and knives well out of children's reach.

- Never leave a child unattended in the bath.

- Always make sure the toilet lid is closed.

How does that match up?

Useful conversion tables

Note that conversions in this book are rounded up or down, rather than being absolutely exact.

Length
1cm = 0.3937in
1in = 2.54cm

Metric	Imperial
1cm	½in
1.5cm	⅝in
2cm	¾in
2.5cm	1in
3cm	1¼in
4cm	1½in
5cm	2in
6cm	2½in
7cm	2¾in
8cm	3in
9cm	3½in
10cm	4in
11cm	4¼in
12cm	4¾in
13cm	5in
14cm	5½in
15cm	6in
16cm	6¼in
17cm	6¾in
18cm	7in
19cm	7½in
20cm	8in
30cm	12in
40cm	16in
50cm	20in
60cm	24in
1m	39in

Distance
1km = ⅔ miles
1 mile = 1.6093km

Metric	Imperial
1km	0.62 miles
2km	1¼ miles
3km	1¾ miles
4km	2½ miles
5km	3¼ miles
6km	3¾ miles
7km	4¼ miles
8km	5 miles
9km	5½ miles
10km	6¼ miles

Weight

1g = 0.0353oz
1kg = 2.2046lb
1oz = 28.35g
1lb = 0.4536kg

Volume

1 litre = 1.76 UK pints (2.11 US pints)
1fl oz = 29.574ml
1 UK pint = 0.5683 litres
1 UK gallon = 4.5461 litres
1 cup = 225ml

Metric	Imperial
30g	1oz
55g	2oz
90g	3oz
115g	4oz
140g	5oz
175g	6oz
200g	7oz
225g	8oz
250g	9oz
280g	10oz
310g	11oz
350g	12oz
375g	13oz
400g	14oz
425g	15oz
430g	15¼oz
450g	1lb
480g	1lb 1oz
680g	1lb 8oz
900g	2lb
1.1kg	2lb 7oz
1.3kg	3lb
1.6kg	3lb 8oz
1.8kg	4lb
2kg	4lb 8oz

Metric	Imperial (UK)	US cup
5ml	1 tsp	
15ml	1 tbsp	
60ml	2fl oz	¼ cup
80ml	2½fl oz	⅓ cup
125ml	4fl oz	½ cup
170ml	5½fl oz	⅔ cup
185ml	6fl oz	¾ cup
225ml	8fl oz	1 cup
310ml	10¾fl oz	1¼ cups
330ml	11¼fl oz	1⅓ cups
375ml	13fl oz	1½ cups
420ml	14½fl oz	1⅔ cups
435ml	15¼fl oz	1¾ cups
500ml	17fl oz	2 cups
560ml	19¼fl oz	2¼ cups
600ml	20¼fl oz	2⅓ cups
625ml	21½fl oz	2½ cups

Temperature

$°C \times 9/5 + 32 = °F$
$°F - 32 \times 5/9 = °C$

°C	°F
0°C	32°F
5°C	41°F
10°C	50°F
15°C	59°F
20°C	68°F
25°C	77°F
30°C	86°F
35°C	95°F
40°C	104°F

Conventional oven temperatures

If you have a fan oven, consult the manufacturer's instructions. In general, reduce the conventional oven temperature by 10–20°C/50–68°F and marginally reduce the cooking time.

Description	°C	°F	Gas mark
Very cool	110°C	225°F	¼
	120°C	250°F	½
Cool	140°C	275°F	1
	150°C	300°F	2
	160°C	325°F	3
Moderate	180°C	350°F	4
Moderately hot	190°C	375°F	5
	200°C	400°F	6
Hot	220°C	425°F	7
	230°C	450°F	8
Very hot	240°	475°F	9

International time zones

Time zones are calculated in bands of longitude, starting at the Greenwich Meridian. There are 24 in all, each about 1,038 miles wide at the equator. Moving from west to east from Greenwich you add an hour for each band, or moving west, you subtract an hour.

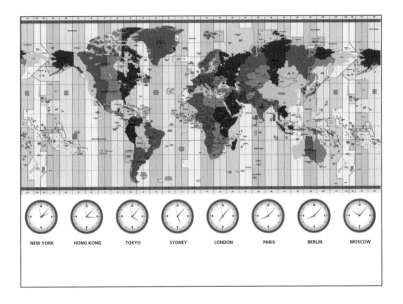

NEW YORK   HONG KONG   TOKYO   SYDNEY   LONDON   PARIS   BERLIN   MOSCOW

Shoe sizes

Shoe sizes in different regions have no exact equivalents, so you may find, for example, that a UK 7 may be called a 40 or a 41.

Europe	UK	US /Canada children	US /Canada women	US /Canada men	Australia	Japan
28	10	10½				17
29	11	11½				18
30	12	12				18.5
31	12½	13				19
32	13½	1				20
33	1	1½				20.5
34	2	2½	4			21
35	3	3	5	3½	3.5	21.5
36	4	4	6	4½	4	22
37	4½	5	6½	5	5	23
38	5½	5½	7½	6	6	23.5
39	6		8½	7	7	24.5
40	7		9	7½	7.5	25
41	7½		9½	8	8	25.5
42	8		10	8½	8.5	26
43	8½		10½	9		27
44	10		12	10½		28
45	11		13	11½		29
46	11½		13½	12		30
47	12		14½	12½		31
48	13		15	13½		32

Children's clothing sizes

Europe	UK	US	Australia	Japan
80cm	12 months	12–18 months	0	80
80–86cm	18 months	18–24 months	1	90
86–92cm	1	1	2	95
92–98cm	2–3	2^T	3	100
98–104cm	3–4	4^T	4	110
104–110cm	4–5	5	5	120
110–116cm	4–6	6	6	
116–122cm	6–7	6–7	7	
122–128cm	7–8	7–8	8	
128–134cm	8–9	9–10	9	
134–140cm	9–10	10	10	
140–146cm	10–11	11	11	
146–152cm	11–12	14	12	

Women's clothing sizes

Metric measurements	Imperial measurements	France, Spain, Portugal	Italy	Germany, Scandinavia	UK/ Australia	US	Japan
71–76cm	28–30in	34	38	32	6	4	5–7
76–81cm	30–32in	36	40	34	8	6	7–9
81–86cm	32–34in	38	42	36	10	8	9–11
86–91cm	34–36in	40	44	38	12	10	11–13
91–97cm	36–38in	42	46	39	14	12	13–15
97–102cm	38–40in	44	48	40	16	14	15–17
102–107cm	40–42in	46	50	42	18	16	17–19
107–112cm	42–44in	48	52	44	20	18	19–21
112–117cm	44–46in	50	54	46	22	20	21–23
117–122cm	46–48in	52	56	48	24	22	23–25

Men's clothing sizes

Men's clothes are generally sold by chest, waist and hip measurements.

Metric	Imperial
Collar sizes	
37mm	14½in
38mm	15in
39mm	15½
40mm	16in
42mm	16½
43mm	17in
44mm	17½
Clothes measurements	
56cm	22in
61cm	24in
66cm	26in
71cm	28in
76cm	30in
81cm	32in
86cm	34in
91cm	36in
96cm	38in
101cm	40in
106cm	42in
111cm	44in
116cm	46in
121cm	48in

Knitting needles

Metric	UK	US
2mm	14	0
2.25mm	13	1
2.75mm	12	2
3mm	11	
3.25mm	10	3
3.75mm	9	5
4mm	8	6
4.5mm	7	7
5mm	6	8
5.5mm	5	9
6mm	4	10
6.5mm	3	10.5
7mm	2	
7.5mm	1	11
8mm	0	12
9mm	00	13
10mm	000	15
12mm		17
15mm		19
20mm		35
50mm		50

Crochet hooks

Metric	UK	US number	US letter
For cotton			
0.6mm	6	1	
0.75mm	5	2	
1mm	4		
1.25mm	3	3	
1.5mm	2.5	5	
1.75mm	2	6	
For wool			
2mm	14	1	B
2.25mm	13	1	B
2.75mm	12	2	C
3.25mm	10	3	D
3.5mm	9	4	E
3.75mm	9	5	F
4mm	8	6	G
4.5mm	7	7	
5mm	6	8	H
5.5mm	5	9	I
6mm	4	10	J
6.5mm	3	101/4	
7mm	2	101/2	K
8mm	0		
9mm	00		
10mm	000		P

EMERGENCY CONTACTS

In a difficult situation, it helps to minimize stress if you can act quickly and get hold of the right people or the right tools for the job. These details may well be on your smartphone, but what's the betting it is out of battery just when you need it. And I'm sure you know your own numbers, but if your neighbours run in to help, they won't know the numbers or the password to your phone. Fill out the following so you have a reference, or draw up your own list of emergency numbers and keep it somewhere prominent.

Quick-reference numbers

My address and postcode ....
....
....
.... Postcode.................................
My landline number.....................................
My mobile number.......................................
Emergency services.....................................
Doctor .... Phone.......................................
Nearest pharmacy .... Phone.......................................
Nearest DIY store .... Phone.......................................
Emergency electrician ....
Emergency plumber ....
Home handyman..

Where to find it

Fuse box..
Lighter/matches..
Stopcock..
Torch ....
Tool box ....